RENEWALS 458-4574
DATE DUE

WITHDRAWN
UTSA Libraries

Thailand in Transition

ASIAN STUDIES AT HAWAII, NO. 32

Thailand in Transition
The Role of Oppositional Forces

Ross Prizzia

CENTER FOR ASIAN AND PACIFIC STUDIES
UNIVERSITY OF HAWAII
UNIVERSITY OF HAWAII PRESS

Copyright © 1985 by University of Hawaii Press
All rights reserved
Manufactured in the United States of America

Library of Congress Cataloging in Publication Data

Prizzia, Ross.
  Thailand in transition

  (Asian studies at Hawaii ; no. 32)
  Includes index.
  1. Thailand—Politics and government. I. Title.
II. Series.
DS3.A2A82   no.32   [DS586]   959.3   85-1059
ISBN 0-8248-0977-7 (pbk.)

Contents

FIGURES AND TABLES		vii
PREFACE		ix
ACKNOWLEDGMENTS		xi
1	INTRODUCTION	1
2	THE COMMUNIST PARTY OF THAILAND	7
3	THE WORKERS	26
4	CATALYSTS OF THE TRANSITION: THE THAI STUDENT MOVEMENT	37
5	THE THAI PARLIAMENT AS AN OPPOSITIONAL FORCE	86
6	THE MEANING OF THAILAND'S TRANSITION	103
INDEX		115

Figures

1	Location of universities in Bangkok	41
2	Structure of the NSCT	49
3	Organization of the NSCT during the five-day protest	66

Tables

1	Incidence of insurgency: 1966–1972	19
2	Danger zones	23
3	Enrollment, year of foundation, and location of Thai universities	39
4	Comparison of election results: 1976 and 1979	97

Preface

Thailand in Transition goes beyond the conventional approach to Thai politics present in most of the literature, which concentrates on the traditional institutions in Thailand—the monarchy, the military, and the bureaucracy. The objective here has been rather to examine the more contemporary emergent oppositional forces struggling to play a permanent and significant role in the broader context of Thai politics.

Oppositional forces in Thailand are many and varied, ranging from the outlawed Communist Party of Thailand (CPT), which seeks to overthrow the Thai government, to the Thai Parliament, which is usually legitimized as part of the government for brief periods between military coups. This book focuses on the CPT, workers, students, and Parliament by presenting in historical perspective the origins, nature, and influence of each as an oppositional force in Thai politics. Special attention is given to the transitional role of these oppositional forces during and after the dramatic shifts in Thai politics precipitated by the student revolution of 1973, the military coup of 1976, the increased hostilities between the People's Republic of China (PRC) and Vietnam in 1979, and the abortive coup by the Thai "Young Turk" military faction in 1981.

A separate chapter is devoted to each of the oppositional forces, which have unique historical backgrounds. The histories of these oppositional forces often transcend domestic Thai politics and involve ideological and other significant influences from the PRC, Vietnam, and the United States. Moreover, these oppositional forces have influenced significant periods of upheaval in contemporary Thai politics and have also affected Thai foreign policy toward the United States, PRC, Vietnam, and to a lesser extent Japan.

It is my contention that the net effect of these upheavals, beginning with the student revolution of 1973, has been the gradual reform of traditional Thai institutions and the development of a fragile but more permanent framework for democratic institutions. Most noteworthy among these democratic institutions are free and regular elections, a viable Parliament, and broad-based political parties.

This struggle and potential for democracy should be of particular interest to even the most casual follower of political events. In the wave of authoritarian regimes of the extreme left and right that has risen and engulfed most of the Southeast Asian countries since 1975, the Philippines included, Thailand remains at a critical political vantage point.

Without the development of permanent democratic institutions Thailand may eventually face a fate similar to that of Laos or Kampuchea. Even with the existence of the Association of Southeast Asian Nations (ASEAN) and the Thai government's various bilateral protection agreements with the United States, PRC, and other countries, the Thais still face the threat of Vietnamese military forces poised along the borders between Thailand and Kampuchea and Laos. In the last analysis, the Thais cannot take much comfort from recent statements of government officials from Singapore and Malaysia who were quoted in various newspapers as saying that Malaysia and Singapore "stand ready to fight the Vietnamese communist forces to the last Thai."

Ross Prizzia

Acknowledgments

The author would like to sincerely thank the following people for reviewing various sections of this book: Boonrak Boonyaketmala of the School of Journalism at Thammasat University, Dr. Robert Scalapino, chairman of the Political Science Department at the University of California at Berkeley, Dr. Ben Kerkvliet, professor of political science at the University of Hawaii, Dr. Walter Vella, professor of Thai history at the University of Hawaii, and Dr. Frank Darling, chairman of the Political Science Department at DePauw University. Special thanks go to Dr. Seymour Martin Lipset, professor of government at Harvard University, who made several useful suggestions regarding the presentation of the first four chapters, and to Dr. Narong Sinsawasdi, professor of political science at Thammasat University, who assisted in the preparation of Chapter 4.

1
Introduction

Transition, as it is implied here, encompasses the important liberalizing changes of the new political environment which emerged in the aftermath of the student revolution of October 1973. Hence transition means more than the relatively liberal provisions and other changes of the new Thai constitution. Constitutional change is not new to Thailand, but the prevailing civilian awareness and attitude toward socialism, as well as the increasing demands by well-organized groups of students, teachers, workers, and farmers, do represent a significant departure from all previous attempts to achieve democracy in Thailand. Successful strikes by workers in Bangkok and grass-roots movements in the provinces have characterized the new emerging forces in Thai politics since the October student revolt of 1973. These political events occurred at a rate never before experienced by the Thais. Moreover, unlike previous protests, these movements gained broad-based support from diverse sectors of Thai society. Thailand's experiment with democracy after 1973 became not only the promotion of democratic institutions but a new determination on the part of previously neglected and suppressed sectors of Thai society to achieve permanent enfranchisement. Transition, in the context of political developments since 1973, is related to three main areas of concern: bureaucratic reform, emerging social forces, and changes in domestic and foreign policy.

CHANGE ON SEVERAL FRONTS

After the 1973 student-led overthrow of the Thanom military regime, Thailand's domestic policies became more involved with socialistic programs representing a new policy approach. Related to this new approach in domestic affairs was the bureaucratic reform which had taken place at various levels of the Thai bureaucracy.

The traditional Thai bureaucracy has persisted in a conventional mold with few exceptions since Prince Damrong instituted the reforms of King Chulalongkorn the Great. This bureaucracy has been described by many scholars of Thai politics (among them F. W. Riggs, W. F. Vella, J. L. Sutton, and W. Siffen) as being one of the most adaptable and, at the same time, the most durable systems of civil service in Southeast Asia. Formed on Confucian principles of civil service and hierarchy of authority that owed its origins and legitimacy to the monarchy, this system has continued almost unchanged since the 1932 coup which legally shifted the bureaucracy from the monarchy to civilian and military control. In the aftermath of the bloodless coup of 1932, power shifted to a slightly broader based decision-making apparatus, but rule by various dominant cliques at the highest level of this new power base still persisted.

In comparison, reforms after October 1973 differed from previous reforms in that the new changes were instigated from below and addressed the process of selection in various sectors of the Thai bureaucracy. Several stabilized positions in the bureaucratic hierarchy of some of the ministries, which were normally based on upward advancement via seniority, became increasingly rotative due to reform-minded Thai intellectuals and the liberal atmosphere in the aftermath of the October revolt. In some cases, a new democratic elective process replaced the traditional appointments. These innovations were tried, began to be accepted at various levels of the government bureaucracy, and became particularly evident in the educational institutions. Although the universities witnessed the most change, the process was attempted by many other institutions including the Ministry of Interior, various council positions, and even upper-level positions of investigative teams involved in cases of government corruption. A variety of techniques were employed to make recruitment and membership in these organizations and government bodies more representative.

Another significant aspect of the transition was the emergence of new social forces. The pressure brought to bear on the provincial administrations in the urban centers outside the capital city of Bangkok became increasingly intense, although organized protests by the proliferation of oppositional groups which emerged after the October 1973 revolt were most intense in Bangkok. The techniques of the new social forces in pressing demands on the various ministries and agencies of the government became as diversified as the demands themselves. In one case a schoolteacher, speaking to a rally of striking teachers in front of the Ministry of Education, cut his wrist to emphasize his determination to remain until the government capitulated to the teachers' demands.

The largest and most visible oppositional force immediately after the 1973 October revolution was the students of the National Student Center of Thailand (NSCT). Other student organizations, such as the Federation of Independent Students of Thailand (FIST), which were breakaway groups from the NSCT, also became prominent in pressing various demands for reform on the new civilian government. In the eight to ten months after the October uprising, however, many other groups assumed an influential role. Fishermen's organizations began to mobilize national support more effectively and press their demands for fishing rights and wage and price guarantees, while farmers' associations conducted marches and also began to organize and play an effective role in trying to achieve land reform and price controls in rice production and distribution. Moreover, other concerned citizens' groups organized strikes and used various techniques to press their demands on the government. At the same time, workers and others became more effective in exerting pressure on the government. Many of their demands were for labor reform and other domestic policies calling for greater control over foreign investments and more equitable distribution of goods and services.

Another characteristic of the transition involved changes in Thailand's foreign policy. This aspect of the transition has most to do with Thailand's ultimate survival in the strategy for peace in Southeast Asia. Accordingly, Thai foreign policy began to shift toward neutralism and nonalignment in its mildest form and toward anti-neocolonialism in its harshest form. The change in Thai foreign policy was also characterized by a general trend toward normalization of relations with the People's Republic of China and accommodation with the new communist governments of Vietnam, Laos, and Kampuchea. Another significant aspect of the foreign policy change was the withdrawal of U.S. troops from Thailand and the general proposals of Thailand's first coalition government. Kukrit Pramoj, who led the coalition government in 1973, devised a policy to phase out most American-backed programs for counterinsurgency and defense support. The overall proposal was designed so that no country in the future would use Thailand as a base for aggression on other countries in Asia. These new policy proposals pertained particularly to the U.S. air force bases which had carried out bombing missions over Laos, Kampuchea, and North Vietnam. This general policy shift included the prohibition of U.S. reconnaisance flights from Thailand over the Indian Ocean. These new far-reaching policies, domestic and international in scope, began to form a pattern of policy objectives which fostered a political climate favorable to the broadening of the base of democracy in Thailand.

The new political climate also helped to foster specific programs designed to maintain democratic institutions. One such program was the Teaching Democracy Program which sent five thousand students to villages in order to work with the people. This program included a public relations component which was aired daily at prime time on national television. It also included a series of colorful posters designed to prepare the *phuu noi* (common people) for democracy. Various posters depicting the necessity of equal treatment for all classes of people generally sought to promote the right of all Thai citizens to participate in the politics and future of their own country. Moreover, the public relations aspect of this program was designed to break down the psychological barriers which had helped keep the rural Thais submissive to authoritarian rule by previous military regimes.

Another element of the transition, though one not likely to play a dominant role in the near future, was the philosophical movement which grew extensively on the left of the Thai political spectrum. Thai leftist intellectuals, representing Marxist and Russian progressivist philosophies, promoted socialistic adaptations to the Thai situation. Moreover, a Maoist movement caught hold among university students who wanted to propagate radical changes in the provinces. Representatives of the Russian philosophical movement proposed programs which would gradually increase the pressure for change on traditional Thai institutions; the Maoist-oriented movement was more interested in inculcating new values in the common people to replace those deemed most resistant to the proposed radical reforms of the Thai political system.

The political environment, particularly after 1973, also created a unity of purpose among many oppositional groups. Students and leftist groups jointly supported the protests against police incursions involving mistreatment of members of separatist movements in southern Thailand. Leaders of regional guerrilla movements in the north and northeast had begun to collaborate in an attempt to create a unified front of insurgency. Moreover, the general publication and leadership of "new left" and traditional communist literature increased a hundredfold during this period. At the universities, Thai intellectuals, instructors, and students began organizing panels, seminars, and study groups to debate various political issues including the relative merits of the Marxist, Maoist, and Russian progressivist approaches to political and economic development.

Democracy in Transition

It should be made clear, however, that it was not communist-supported movements for a "people's democracy" or a "new democracy" that characterized political change in Thailand either during the liberal period from 1973 to 1976 or during the right-wing regime of Thanin from 1976 to 1979. Neither is the term "democracy" when used in the context of transition meant to imply only a reemergence of elections and parliamentary government.

Democracy in this context goes beyond the growth of democratic and parliamentary forms and addresses itself liberally to a "broadening of the base"—the enfranchisement of new groups. It is the expansion of popular participation in a largely autocratic decision-making structure. While such a process may admittedly occur within an authoritarian or totalitarian system, what makes Thailand's democracy unique is that the Thais have chosen to broaden their political base through the mechanism of parliamentarianism. By retaining accepted Thai values whenever possible—despite their denunciation by some elements—in conjunction with Western vehicles for popular representation, the Thais have blended Eastern methods with Western forms.

Hence students could overthrow an unpopular regime and call for a government of the masses, all the while prominently displaying portraits of the monarchy's incumbents, the king and queen. Volunteers could take to the countryside in an attempt to foster a Maoist cultural revolution of sorts, but parliamentary democracy was the intended beneficiary. And workers could use Soviet methods designed to achieve power for the workers—not in order to seize the means of production but rather for the capitalist end of higher wages.

After 1973 a new system emerged with the embryo of a new popular consensus buttressing the legitimacy of parliamentary forms. Between October 1973 and October 1976 hundreds of incidents occurred throughout the kingdom, any one of which would in the era of military domination have served as justification for a coup. Emergent opposition forces forestalled such a happening, and it is with the roots and growth of this kind of democracy and participation that this book is concerned.

The Opposition

In Thailand oppositional forces are viewed as groups of people mobilized to oppose or change the Thai government as represented by the monarch, the bureaucratic elite, and the military. Opposition can take the form of parliamentary opposition, which has been legitimized for brief periods between military coups, or it may take a more violent form such as that of the Communist Party of Thailand. Between these two extremes various groups have emerged to oppose the Thai government on specific issues and for particular periods of time. It is not my intention to identify and explain the nature of all these groups; instead I shall focus on two of the broad-based "progressive forces" which gained significant momentum during and after the student revolution of 1973: workers and students.

Other significant oppositional groups, such as the separatist movement of the Malay Thais in the south and the Meo tribes in the north, have been reasonably successful in sustaining their movements for relatively long periods of time. These oppositional groups are regional and ethnic in origin and nature, however, and are seen as oppositional forces only within the broad context of the Communist Party of Thailand (CPT).

This book deals only with those Thai oppositional forces represented by the CPT, workers, students, and Parliament. In the following pages I shall explain the origin, nature, and influence of each in Thai politics.

2
The Communist Party of Thailand

The Communist Party of Thailand (CPT) can be traced as far back as 1925, when a Chinese communist agent was sent to organize overseas Chinese in Thailand. The Nationalist Chinese Party, the Kuomintang, had already set up many similar organizations among the Chinese workers in Bangkok. After the split between the Chinese communists and the Kuomintang in China in 1927, similar ideological disagreements developed among the overseas Chinese in Thailand. Chinese communists in Thailand began to break away from the various overseas Chinese organizations formed by the Kuomintang. At about the same time, many university students had been introduced to the ideas of Marx by European instructors at Chinese universities.

When serious differences arose between the Kuomintang and the Communist Party in China, many of these Marxist-oriented university students were arrested by order of Kuomintang officials. To escape arrest, many students fled to Thailand where they helped to organize the communist movement. Under their leadership, various new organizations were initiated. The most important of these new communist groups was the Association of Communist Youth of Siam, which sought to spread the ideas of Marx and Lenin, increase party membership, and raise funds to support the communists' struggle against the Kuomintang in China.

THE INFLUENCE OF HO CHI MINH

From 1928 to 1931, according to some sources, the communist movement in Thailand gained momentum from the Vietnamese Communist

Party under the leadership of Ho Chi Minh. According to a biography of Ho Chi Minh written by Jean Lacoutre, Ho worked with the Vietnamese community in Thailand to strengthen the struggle for independence from France.[1] Lacoutre maintains that Ho Chi Minh had considerable influence in the eventual development of communism in northeastern Thailand and in the resistance of Buddhist monks to the Saigon government:

> The following autumn Ho sailed from Siam with a triple objective: to set up cells among the substantial Vietnamese colony there; to foment trouble at the expense of the administration in nearby Indochina; and to reorganize the Comintern's networks in Southeast Asia. In November 1928, there began to be talk of a certain "Old Chin" in the northeastern provinces of Siam. He was rumored to have come from China. But the Vietnamese in Siam saw quickly that he was one of their own people. In Udong, and subsequently in Sakon Nakhon, he founded a newspaper called *Thanh-Ai* (Friendship), opened a school where Vietnamese and Thai were taught side by side, and set up a forest cooperative. The villagers worshiped "The Lord High Genie Tran"—the departed spirit of Tran Hung Dao, the legendary sovereign who had defeated the Mongols; so "Old Chin" composed a song of praise to the "guardian spirit of the mountains and waters of Vietnam": requirements of the "nationalist phase" were leading him onto strange ground. But in the eyes of Nguyen Ai Quoc, or Vuong, or Chin [the various names of Ho Chi Minh], anything that extolled the country's merits was paving the way for revolution.
>
> Clad in the robes of a Buddhist monk, he afterwards lived for a while in Bangkok, studying and preaching and at the same time setting up cells within the pagodas, training the young monks in a comprehensive social philosophy which embraced everything except the foreign invader and his hirelings. Traces of the networks which he then established, and of the watchwords which he imparted, came to light years afterwards in south and southeastern Cochin China (1945), and perhaps even in 1963–1966, when the Buddhists rose against the authorities in Saigon. After all, Buddhism is rooted in attachment to the land of one's fathers. It attaches importance to the real, the immediate, the given, the experienced. It is a happy hunting-ground for a skilled Marxist like Ho.[2]

By 1931, the Vietnamese Communist Party (VCP) had moved its headquarters from Vietnam to northeastern Thailand to seek the cooperation of the Vietnamese living there. The VCP workers were particularly effective in finding sympathizers among the Thai Vietnamese, overseas Chinese, and Thai students.

After the 1932 revolution, in which the absolute monarchy was overthrown in a bloodless coup organized by the military and Pridi

Panomyong, the Thai communists increased their propaganda under the name Siam Communist Committee. This group claimed some credit for the change in government and removal of the absolute powers of the monarchy. About this time, three newspapers emerged which supported the claims of the Siam Communist Committee. Their names carried symbolic revolutionary titles: *Satjang* (Truth), *24 Mithuna* (24 June—the date of the revolution), and *Muanchom Risapda* (Masses Weekly), all of which gave Marxist interpretations of international events.

The liberal political atmosphere which was so prevalent in 1932 soon disappeared, and in 1933 the Thai government passed the first anticommunist law. The law did not deter several young advocates of socialism, however, for the very next year leaflets urging the establishment of a Russian-style government in Thailand were distributed in the northeast by university students under the name of Khananum Thai (Thai Youth Group). In 1935, the Thai government strengthened its anticommunist stand and further amended the anticommunist statute of 1933 to deal with the emergence of communist groups under noncommunist names.

The invasion of China by Japan caused many anticommunist leaders in China and Southeast Asia to seek the aid of indigenous communists. From 1935 to 1941, there began a general trend of anti-Japanese alliances in Southeast Asia among nationalists and communists alike. After 1941, many communists entered Thailand to fight the common enemy Japan.

It was at this time that the Thai Communist Party (TCP) was officially established and in the name of "Thai patriotism" announced its support of the Free Thai Movement. The Free Thai Movement was a group of Thai patriots who continued to resist Japanese occupation after the Thai government, under Prime Minister Phibun, had declared war against the United States in collaboration with the Japanese and their goals for Southeast Asia. The Free Thai Movement was not a fighting force as was the French Resistance in Europe; its primary purpose was to supply information on Japanese plans and installations in Thailand to the allies. It was originally organized by Pridi Panomyong in collaboration with the allied intelligence unit, the Office of Strategic Services (OSS).[3] The Thai government and the Japanese administrators were aware of the existence of the Free Thai Movement but tolerated its activities for the sake of the war effort. A case in point is Dr. Puay Ungphakorn, who was parachuted by the OSS into northern Thailand to support the Free Thai Movement. Although captured and imprisoned for his activities, Puay was released from jail every night in order to continue his work.

During this period (1941–1945), the Thai Communist Party became an effective part of the anti-Japanese alliance. The TCP expanded its activities and divided the party organization into two independent branches: a Chinese Executive Committee, primarily comprised of Thai Chinese, and a Thai Executive Committee made up of indigenous Thais.

The favorable political climate for the TCP's activities was sustained even after the war. Some political observers attributed this situation to the need of the Thai government to court the USSR in order to obtain approval for membership in the United Nations. Thus, in 1946, when the Thai government abolished all anticommunist acts, the Chinese branch of the TCP severed itself completely from the parent organization under the name Chinese Communist Party of Thailand (CCPT) and began recruiting left-leaning Chinese from the overseas Chinese communities in Bangkok and Thonburi. The main concern of the CCPT was still to support the Chinese Communist Party's struggle in mainland China. Under the new organizational name and a more effective party apparatus, the CCPT gained considerable influence over the Thai Chinese community. The weekly publication of *Mahachon* (The Great Mass) greatly assisted the CCPT in its efforts to increase membership among students and laborers in the rural areas. By 1947, however, the Thai government, having obtained membership in the United Nations with considerable support from the United States, began once again to suppress the communist movement, and overseas Chinese became the target of government harassment in the form of deportation, school closure, and press censorship. After the successful coup d'etat by Phibun Songkham, the communists were forced to move underground.

In 1949, after the victory by the communists in China, the Chinese Communist Party of Thailand ceased most of its activities. Most of the members of the CCPT went to China while others joined the Thai Communist Party. In the meantime, United States programs for aid and defense support began to move in and consolidate the U.S. position with the Thai military leaders. In 1950, the Thai communists attempted to cooperate with various civilian leaders and politicians in hopes of mounting a successful countercoup. The attempt failed, and it was the last time the Thai Communist Party tried to achieve its aims through parliamentary means. Thereafter the TCP leadership advocated "armed struggle" and a "people's war."

A clandestine organization, the Thai Liberation Organization, was formed and its members were sent to communist-controlled areas of Vietnam and Laos for training. The next year, 1951, at a meeting of all communist representatives, the party's name was officially changed from the Thai Communist Party to the Communist Party of Thailand

(CPT). Generally the party's official policy was a carbon copy of the strategy put forth by Mao Tse-tung. Members of the CPT were called upon to support revolution by violent means or by protracted warfare via a strategy which would first liberate the masses in the rural areas and thereby enable them to surround the cities. By December of 1952, this policy began to be put into action by the party's front organization, the Thai Liberation Organization (TLO). The TLO organized what later came to be called a "Peace Revolt." This initial attempt at open confrontation with the government was a complete failure and most of the TLO leaders were arrested. Thereafter the Thai government revitalized its efforts against the communist movement and enacted an anticommunist law calling for more severe punishment for members of communist organizations. The CPT was forced to disband the TLO and curtail all plans for expansion as the government began arresting CPT members and sympathizers in considerable numbers. It was during this time that the socialist author Kularb Saipradit was arrested.

Rather than attempt further expansion in Thailand, the CPT then began sending most of its remaining members to China for training. In 1953, the CPT set up three organizations for general assistance, infiltration, and recruitment. Although these organizations had names designated by the CPT, they came to be known by the names given them by the Thai government's Communist Suppression Operations Command (CSOC): the Gray Organization, the Yellow Organization, and the Red Organization. The Gray Organization was a front organization of semi-legal status that included groups for helping laborers, the Temple Committee, the Household Medicine Committee (first aid), various musical bands, sports teams, and student tutorial units. The Yellow Organization was designed for infiltration into various government-sponsored groups for working with all persons opposed to the government, such as the Thai Labor Association. The Red Organization was the unit for politicization and party recruitment; in turn it formed such groups as the United Professional Workers' Union, the Thai Liberation Organization, the Farmers' Liberation Organization, and the Thai Youth Organization.

These organizations continued their clandestine activities until the general election of 1957, when the CPT was able to initiate contact with progressive Thai politicians who had won seats in the new Parliament. Since many of these politicians were in agreement with policies of socialism and anti-imperialism, the CPT grasped the opportunity to use these contacts to transfer a considerable number of their operatives from the countryside to the cities. The CPT's strategy was based on the hope that vital political contacts in Bangkok would assist their overall efforts in increasing financial and political support for their bases in the rural areas.

These plans were aborted in 1958, when the fervent anticommunist Sarit Thanarat led a successful coup and assumed control over the newly formed government. With the help of various U.S.-supported agencies, Sarit initiated a series of counterinsurgency operations.[4] Faced with this new anticommunist push, many of the socialist-oriented politicians in Bangkok disassociated themselves from the CPT while others found refuge as professors at universities in the provinces. The University of Chiang Mai became a popular haven for the students of Pridi and supporters of socialist reform. There were a few intellectuals who remained quietly at their posts in the faculty of economics at Thammasat University; several other professors sought refuge abroad. It was during this time that Kularb Saipradit, after spending more than five years in confinement as a political prisoner, requested and was granted political asylum in Peking.

In view of the sudden change in the political situation, the CPT was forced to revert to its initial objectives of working primarily in the provinces. With Sarit in power and U.S. military assistance increasing at an unprecedented rate, the CPT apparently realized that the situation was still unsuitable for a real "people's war." The CPT subsequently discarded many of the strategies employed before the Sarit coup and concentrated instead on building an infrastructure of highly qualified cadres in the provincial and village administrations. Many problems arose in the early stages of implementing the new strategy, however, because many of the provincial party members were not well versed in the CPT's principles and consequently their effectiveness was negligible.

By 1961, the CPT had altered its strategy to accommodate the use of armed resistance once again. To this end, a new front organization was established—the Democratic Patriotic Front. This new organization sought territorial acquisition through protracted warfare in suitable areas of provincial Thailand. From 1961 to 1964, the Democratic Patriotic Front concentrated its efforts in northeastern Thailand and was eventually successful in seizing remote parts of Nakhon Phanom and Sakhon Nakhon provinces, which were utilized as support bases. These bases supported the overall strategy of the CPT, which was to avoid direct confrontation with government troops and provincial officers while concentrating its resources exclusively upon the formation and training of effective fighting units.

In 1964, the CPT formed a new organization, the Volunteer Liberation Organization (VLO), to recruit and train members and about the same time established the Movement for the Independence of Thailand (MIT). After the establishment of the MIT, its leaders announced a return to a previous strategy—that of using the cities as a means of supporting CPT activities in the rural areas. Having been able to establish several fighting units in northeastern Thailand, the CPT also adjusted its strategy regarding confrontation with the government forces and began to encourage expansion through armed struggle in the provinces. Thereafter localized and limited warfare frequently occurred between various communist fighting units and government forces in the remote villages of the provinces throughout the countryside. In August of 1965, the Thai Patriotic Front engaged the government forces in a fierce battle at Baan Na Bua village in the province of Nakhon Phanom. Though the communists suffered serious losses in this battle, further clashes continued at Phuksed Mountain in Ubon Ratchathani province and various villages in the northern provinces of Nan, Pitsanulok, Phetchabun, Uttaradit, Tak, and Chiengrai. The armed struggle spread as fighting broke out in the southern provinces of Surat Thani, Nakhon si Thammarat, and Phattalung and eventually penetrated areas just south of Bangkok in the provinces of Ratchaburi, Phetburi, and Prachuap Khiri Khan. It was also during this period beginning in 1964 that the People's Republic of China's official statements began lending support to the CPT.

CHINA AND THE CPT

Although the People's Republic of China (PRC) played a role in the training of cadres for the CPT and provided a haven for an ideological assortment of Thai exiles, the Chinese Community Party (CCP) was relatively silent in giving official recognition to the CPT. The PRC's official position changed somewhat in 1964, however, when the CCP issued a National Day congratulatory message to the CPT. Without mentioning the Soviet Union by name, the message implied an allegiance to revolution in the CCP image, and not by the means of "revisionist forces" who had "betrayed the meaning of revolution."[5] Moreover, the message promised that "the relationships between the peoples of the two countries will grow closer and closer."[6] The message also attacked the Royal Thai Government's "hostile policy toward China" and maintained that the Thanom government was nothing more than a "slavish tool" of the U.S. imperialists.[7]

It became apparent that the CPT had chosen alliance with the CCP and had adopted a Maoist approach to revolution. This was not really surprising, of course, since the so-called philosophers of Thai socialism were exiled in China during this time. It should be noted, however, that the writings of Pridi and Kularb Saipradit, two of the most prominent Thai socialist philosophers exiled in China, reflected aspects of Russian progressivist philosophy which allowed for cultural adaptations and gradual change of the system. Pridi wrote *The Impermanence of Society* while in China. Published in Thai (*Kwam Pen Annicang Khong Sangkhom*) in 1957, it generally reflects Pridi's attempts to synthesize Buddhist theological precepts and Marxist dialectics. Kularb Saipradit's *Till We Meet Again* (*Chon Ca Phoop Kan Mai*) is considered vulgar by some Thai scholars because of Kularb's common use of idiomatic expressions from the Thai marketplace. Other Thai intellects, however, regard Kularb's adaptations to the language of the *phuu noi* humanistic and appropriate. Because of his writings and firm commitment to the socialist cause, Kularb is generally more highly regarded than Pridi by many Thai intellectuals.

The CPT's 1964 message was uncompromising and called for a united front to be formed from below to overthrow the Thai government. There were other, and perhaps more basic, reasons why the grass-roots approach to revolution, the Maoist approach, seemed appropriate for Thailand. First of all, political parties were outlawed during this period (1959–1967), and forms of overt political participation were precluded for most Thai. Moreover, the leadership and cadre levels of the CPT were still primarily comprised of Thai-Chinese and northeastern Thai of Laotian and Vietnamese origin. Pridi, though respected, was basically an ethnic Thai, and it is generally believed that while Pridi was in Peking he interacted very little with the Thai-Chinese CPT representatives. Although Pridi reportedly authored several articles for the CCP newspaper *Jen-min-jih-Pao* in the 1950s, other Thai exiles such as Monkon Nonakon, who was imprisoned for subversion, emerged to lead the MIT. Pridi apparently played only a ceremonial, if sometimes obscure, leadership role. Even Kularb Saipradit, though quite old, was more active than Pridi in the CPT while in China. Kularb was often mentioned as a Thai delegate to various CCP-sponsored international front conferences and was generally more involved in CPT international activities than was Pridi. Another exile, Phayom Chulanond, also emerged in a role of leadership to the MIT and the Thai Patriotic Front (TPF), but he is often described by Thai as being more "opportunist than communist." Phayom was an M.P. from Phet Buri to the Thai Parliament from 1948 to 1950. He failed at reelection in 1950, so he reentered the Thai army where he achieved the rank of lieutenant colonel until it was stripped from him by the Thai government in 1964.[8] Regardless of the image of Phayom as a "frustrated opportunist" projected by several Thai officials (Thanat Khoman, for example), as of 1971 he was believed to have remained a member of the TPF's central committee and this organization's official "overseas representative."⁹

In 1965, several Thai delegations representing these newly formed front organizations (among them the Thai Patriotic Front) began to surface at various conferences in Peking. These included a Thailand Federation of Patriotic Workers, a Thai Afro-Asian Solidarity Committee, and a Thailand Federation of Trade Unions.[10]

According to some sources, the training of Thai leftists for political indoctrination at the Marxist-Leninist Institute in Peking began to increase during this period (1964–1965). However, it is generally believed that even with the increased activities in Peking and at the cadre training school in K'un-ming (Yunnan province), the total number of Thai trainees in China was small compared to the number trained in North Vietnam.[11]

NORTH VIETNAM AND THE CPT

While China was training relatively few senior Thai cadres (approximately seven hundred between 1952 and 1969), North Vietnam, beginning around 1962, began "graduating" more than a hundred Thai and Thai-Lao each year from the Hoa Binh School near Hanoi.[12] Apparently China and North Vietnam had established a division of labor for training programs: The Chinese provided indoctrination and training to prepare the higher-ranking members of the CPT; the North Vietnamese provided training and equipment in preparing ordinary soldiers and low-level cadres for the revolution. Since most of the Thai trainees in North Vietnam were either Thai-Lao or Thai-Vietnamese, there is considerable speculation that many of these graduates were sent to Laos to assist the communist Pathet Lao rather than back to Thailand to join the CPT.[13] This division of labor in which the Chinese trained the leadership while the North Vietnamese trained low-level cadres and ordinary soldiers persisted until 1976 when major differences between China and North Vietnam caused serious problems of unity for the CPT.

The year 1965 was an ideological milestone for the CPT as the objectives for a people's revolution became more apparent. The shift in CPT policy in directing all fighting units to engage in armed struggle was combined with a well-defined twelve-point program drawn up by the CPT's Revolutionary People's Council. The various points were enumerated as follows:

1. To destroy the Thai government and throw out the U.S. imperialists
2. To change the country's policy of reliance upon the United States and to withdraw from SEATO (Southeast Asian Treaty Organization)

3. To set up a new Parliament with representatives drawn from diverse patriotic groups and to formulate a new constitution
4. To guarantee its people basic freedoms of speech, writing, communications, religious belief, meeting and assembly, association, and political parties
5. To ensure that every nationality and race has equal rights
6. To ensure that men and women have equality in political, legal, economic, and social terms
7. To improve the living conditions of the laboring classes
8. To initiate a land reform and improve farmers' living conditions
9. To improve the situation of low-ranking government officials
10. To suppress all forms of corruption and abolish every financial pressure group
11. To abolish the system of monopolistic practices and accelerate the nation's economic development
12. To protect and promote education and native customs

The program carried with it a propaganda offensive designed to destroy all forms of exploitation by imperialists, landlords, and capitalists. The CPT maintained in its message to the Thai people that Thailand had remained under a system of feudalism for the last hundred years. Spokesmen for the CPT argued that:

> Those who have power have always controlled the land while those who produce—the farmers—are exploited by the landlords. Since farmers have little political knowledge or education, attempts at rebellion or demonstration have so far failed, for they did not have the Communist Party and the proletariat as their leaders. When Western capitalist influence penetrated Thailand, the country became a semifeudal quasi-colony. Following the Second World War, all the big powers tried to destroy the emerging national economy through imperialism; the capitalists with their financial powers exploit the people whose only power lies in their own labor. The USA, particularly, tried very hard to promote this form of bondage; the Americans sent USOM to advise and manage all matters of development and technical advance; they sent JUSMAG to control Thailand's military; and they sent USIS and the Peace Corps to supervise and control Thailand's educational and cultural development. The Thai government thus became a puppet of the USA and the Thai people slaves. As Thais we have no freedoms. The Thai government has no stable economic policy for crises in the national economy which will continue to constantly recur, causing a great deal of suffering and injustice to the common, ordinary people.[14]

The CPT's solution to this scenario is a revolution to eliminate all class distinctions in Thai society. According to the CPT, Thai society can be divided into four classes: laborers, farmers, small capitalists, and national capitalists. The CPT defined each group as follows:

1. Although the labor class is still a small group, the laborers are the most exploited and have nothing to lose in supporting revolutionary change. Labor is the most progressive and important group in the revolution.
2. Farmers can be divided into three groups. *Poor farmers* are those who have to rent all their land. They can be treated in the same manner as the labor class. They are exploited in every way and can be relied upon as much as laborers in promoting the revolution. *Middle farmers* have slightly better economic conditions than the poor farmers but they too are exploited by the landlords, capitalists, feudalists, and aristocracy. Although their ideas and potential are not necessarily as progressive as those of the poor farmers, they can be considered good friends and allies. *Rich farmers* are capitalists in the rural sector, often building up their fortunes by exploiting middle and poor farmers; yet they, in turn, are under the power and control of the feudalists, capitalists, and aristocracy. This group also wants independence from its oppressors and may give some support to the revolution.
3. The small capitalists or petite bourgeoisie are teachers, instructors, university professors, university students, and scholars. They too are being exploited and oppressed and are also potential revolutionaries, but they lack the ability to conduct and lead the revolution. Although well connected to the present economic structure, they can nevertheless become allies under the leadership of the proletariat.
4. National capitalists, no matter how rich, are still being exploited by taxation and corruption from the U.S. imperialists. All these groups can be used only when the revolution has progressed to some extent.

To operationalize the CPT policy as it pertained to class distinctions, the party proposed organization of different groups to oppose imperialism, feudalism, landlords, and capitalists. The CPT maintained that these oppositional groups would hasten the growth of socialism and eventually communism.

The CPT firmly established the principle that force must be used to achieve the ultimate victory for the revolution, because "no ruling class in the world will give up its powers willingly and voluntarily."[15] Moreover, the CPT in 1965 reemphasized that parliamentary government will never be able to create equality or promote the interests of the working class, because "Parliament is itself but a reflection of the interests of the ruling class." Therefore the CPT maintained in its 1965 manifesto that "the struggle must involve the use of armed fighting units and political campaigns simultaneously.... The fight must be waged both in towns and in the countryside.... The cities can be surrounded." Moreover, the CPT proposed that the cities should no longer be ignored by the cadres because "much work must be done within the cities to mobilize the laboring classes and organizations need to be created to provide training and political education." Even the various front organizations of the CPT (the Democratic Patriotic Front, for example) established in the early 1960s were in need of training and were largely ineffective prior to 1965. In an attempt to remedy the rather weak condition of the front organization, the Thai Patriotic Front announced a six-point program on 23 January 1965. The program urged all true Thai patriots to:

1. Fight for the independence of the nation and terminate the U.S. connection.
2. Fight for political freedoms and the announcement of a new constitution.
3. Initiate a policy of peace and independence and withdraw from SEATO.
4. Promote economic development, especially of farmers.
5. Improve the methods of punishing corrupt officials and initiate land reform.
6. Improve health and education services and put a stop to the debilitating culture of imperialism.[16]

Also in 1965, a CPT front organization, the Farmers' Liberation Association, put forth its objectives in a six-point program:

1. To gather the collective powers of the farmers
2. To wipe out all traces of U.S. imperialism and that of other Western countries
3. To set up a government with members drawn from among the farmers
4. To protect the rights and benefits of all the people
5. To improve the techniques used in agriculture
6. To struggle to eradicate all class distinctions from society[17]

To operationalize its manifesto and the propaganda statements of its front organizations, the CPT proposed in 1965 a specific plan for recruitment. The CPT maintained that to accomplish the goals of the revolution cadres must become the true friends of the people. To this end, a program of assistance was established which called upon cadres to assist villagers in building their houses, harvesting their crops, and plowing the land. According to the CPT, this rural people-oriented approach would aid the overall program of recruitment.[18] The CPT also reemphasized the three guiding principles on recruitment:

1. Since it takes a long time to mobilize people, the cadres must use great patience, for the poor have been oppressed for so long that they no longer possess self-confidence.

Table 1
Incidence of Insurgency: 1966–1972

Nature of Incident	1966	1967	1968	1969	1970	1971	1972
Fighting	155	232	362	290	258	365	680
Attacks	0	5	5	5	37	36	57
Ambushes	10	21	48	57	53	106	111
Provocations	47	109	226	322	214	217	487
Psychological warfare and propaganda	112	133	73	47	50	88	47
Intimidation	170	154	213	201	332	420	411
Sabotage	11	7	12	7	11	12	57
Shooting	3	5	33	39	30	60	108
Forced logistic support	39	112	102	59	32	46	68
Communists killed	93	182	141	109	96	190	362
Communists arrested	1,440	1,260	613	226	326	713	1,132
Communists surrendered	1,458	693	554	384	191	834	899

2. Cadres must firmly believe that the revolution is for and of the people; it is their revolution. This revolution must occur from contradictions within each village, not from outside means.
3. Propaganda efforts must be adapted to suit the particular localities. The revolution and struggle will occur only if there is some special problem.

It was during the period of 1965–1968, that all organizations were unified under the Thai Patriotic Front and a clandestine "people's network" was established and directed against Americans in Thailand.

The CPT sought to consolidate the Farmers' Liberation Association and all other front organizations throughout the country under the Thai Patriotic Front (TPF) and on 4 January 1969 officially established the People's Liberation Army of Thailand (PLAT). While clandestine radio stations monitored from southern China and communist-controlled areas of Laos continued to denounce the Thai government as "lackeys and running dogs of American imperialism" during this period (1968–1972), the CPT placed less emphasis on propaganda and a greater concentration on acts of violence against the Thai government. Table 1 indicates the extent of the increase in communist activities during the period 1966–1972.[19]

As the insurgents' success in the armed struggle for remote areas of northern Thailand increased at an unprecedented rate, the statistics of death began to favor the communist fighting units throughout the country. Moreover, the ratio of government officials killed to insurgents killed dropped from 1:2.8 in 1967 to 1:0.7 in 1972.[20] The sharp increase in the incidence of insurgency was combined with a CPT effort to intensify the armed struggle in support of the expansion of local fighting units throughout the country.

AFTER THE STUDENT REVOLT

Incidents of insurgency—and the CPT's overall strength—increased at a dramatic rate in the aftermath of the student revolt of 1973. Communist insurgents under arms increased from an estimated 3,500 in 1973 to 5,000 in 1974 and to 8,000 in 1975. The CPT was particularly successful in increasing its strength in northern and northeastern Thailand, but significant increases were also recorded in the central plain and in the southern provinces bordering Burma and Malaysia.

Moreover, the dramatic increase in number of insurgents was apparently combined with a new sophistication of weapons. By mid-1975, almost all insurgents were armed with the latest model of the AK-47 or M-16 rifles, while some units possessed mortars and B-40 rockets similar to those used by the insurgents in Vietnam. The "fighting units" of the insurgent forces also increased in size, and assaults which previously lasted for only a few minutes began to last hours or even longer. Government casualties continued to be more than 50 percent higher than insurgent losses in most of these battles. Similar attacks continued until 1976, when dramatic changes in the leadership and tactics of the Thai government caused the CPT to change its strategy.

The period 1973–1976 marked an unprecedented proliferation of protest groups. Farmers, workers, and students had for the first time an organizational base and a political environment of mobilization and protest which lasted longer than any such period in Thai history. This extended period of liberalization came to an abrupt halt in October 1976 when a bloody battle involving radical students at Thammasat University gave rise to the extreme right-wing government of Thanin Kraivixien. Thanin's subsequent suppression of all outspoken members of the new "progressive" forces caused many to flee to the jungle seeking refuge. The CPT seized this opportunity to woo many of the outcast and disillusioned leaders of the various oppositional forces to join in the creation of a new front organization called the Committee for Coordinating Patriotic and Democratic Forces (CCPDF). The CPT was particularly successful in recruiting well-known activists among the farmers, workers, students, and the outlawed Socialist Party of Thailand to join the CCPDF.

Labor leader Therdphun Chaidee, student activist leaders Thirayuth Bonmee and Seksan Prasertjul, and a former M.P. from the northeast,

Thongpak Priangvat, gave the CCPDF the credibility of being more broad-based than any other front organization created by the CPT in the past. These leaders were not obscure Thais in exile but rather people who were played up in the media as heroes during the 1973–1976 period. In contrast to previous CPT drives to establish fronts, the CCPDF included the creation of international links with Thais abroad and sympathetic foreigners. These new groups, formed primarily in the United States and Europe, demanded a return to democracy and an end to the repressive regime of Thanin.

The CPT's success in these efforts was short-lived because of dramatic shifts in internal and external events. Internally, the Thai government shifted to the more moderate regime of Kriangsak Chamanand and called for elections which eventually took place in April 1979. Externally, China invaded Vietnam over differences regarding Kampuchea. The latter event and the subsequent hostilities between the Chinese and Vietnamese communists caused a kind of schizophrenia for the CPT with regard to origin, loyalties, and strategy.

Already faced with the enormous organizational problem of the new recruits of the broad-based CCPDF, many of whom were not communist or even socialist, the CPT was now confronted with a choice between the Chinese versus Vietnamese connection. This problem was further complicated by factions within the CPT's Thai-Lao communist units of the northeast, many of whom received their training in Hanoi. At first it seemed as if the Chinese faction would prevail, since the leadership of the CPT central committee was still dominated by Chinese-trained cadres. However, the CCPDF's socialist and communist members were split into Chinese-oriented and Vietnamese-oriented factions. When Vietnam invaded Kampuchea in 1978, the CCPDF initially took a "united Thai" position against Vietnamese expansionism and even offered, through the Voice of the People of Thailand (VOPT), to cooperate with the Thai government in order to resist the Vietnamese. But when China invaded Vietnam, the pro-Vietnamese factions among the CCPDF demanded an end to the anti-Vietnam propaganda. In 1979 the CPT, in a new effort to hold a neutral posture in the dispute between China and Vietnam, began to play down the VOPT's denunciations of Vietnam. The Chinese communists responded by closing down the VOPT, which was based in southern China, and ending abruptly the most effective CPT radio broadcasts.

On the other hand, the pro-Peking faction of the CPT, which had for ten years used border areas in Laos as a sanctuary and supply route in its skirmishes with the Thai counterinsurgency, was ordered by the Vietnamese-backed Lao government to return to Thailand and stay out of Laos. The matter became further complicated for the Chinese faction of the CPT in view of the increasingly close ties between the PRC and the "imperialist" government of the United States. After considerable soul-searching and debate, the Chinese factions of the CPT and CCPDF declared that they were not pro-Peking and would act independently of mainland Chinese directives. The new pro-Hanoi factions of the CPT and CCPDF, likewise, claimed that indigenous Thai interests would take precedence over Vietnamese interests.

Regardless of the disclaimers offered by both factions, the old-line pro-Chinese faction has continued to pursue a Maoist-oriented struggle in the rural regions, while the newer and relatively younger pro-Vietnamese factions drawn primarily from the outcasts of the 1976 coup have pursued a new strategy of influence and sabotage in the urban areas of Thailand. The latter strategy has been followed by the pro-Vietnamese faction ever since the CPT's unsuccessful efforts to disrupt the elections of April 1979. During the 1979 election campaigns, the government officially recognized communist influence in rural areas and designated 931 "danger zones." Candidates insisting on campaigning in these areas were required to give a 48-hour advance notice to district officers. Table 2 provides a breakdown of the number of danger zones by region and province.[21]

Even with the split between the pro-Hanoi and pro-Peking forces within the CPT, militarily the Thai People's Liberation Army in 1979 remained around thirteen thousand strong and, up to 1980, seemed able to enlist new recruits in excess of losses. Incidence of insurgency increased dramatically from 1973 to 1979 but dropped significantly in 1980–1981. Moreover, according to Thai government sources the armed guerrillas decreased from thirteen thousand in 1979–1980 to ten thousand in 1980–1981. There is much speculation that this drop in numbers was due as much to the split in the CPT as it was to the new counterinsurgency measures of the Thai government. Perceiving this new split in the CPT as a dual threat, the Thai government under Prem Tinsulamond responded with an "open arms" program which by July 1981 was successful in encouraging the defection of nearly half the estimated four thousand dissidents who joined the CPT movement in 1976. Most of these defectors were radical elements of the labor unions (such as Therdphun), the farmers and students, and the Socialist Party of Thailand and included prominent figures in the pro-Hanoi faction of the CCPDF such as Thirayuth and Seksan.[22]

The "open arms" program is only one aspect of a broad-based counterinsurgency effort conceived by General Saiyud Kerdpol which also includes the CPM (Civil-Police-Military) joint operations concept, var-

Table 2
Danger Zones

Province	Region	Number of Dangerous Areas
Loei	NE	162
Nakhon	NE	123
Ubon Ratchathani	NE	52
Chiyaphum	NE	50
Roi Et	NE	43
Nakhon si Thammarat	S	42
Phattalung	S	42
Buri Ram	NE	40
Surin	NE	36
Khon Kaen	NE	33
Surat Thani	S	32
Mae Hong Son	N	29
Samut Prakan	C	27
Phetchabun	C	22
Phrayao	N	21
Ratchaburi	S	20
Nakhon Sawan	C	20
Uttaradit	N	19
Nan	N	18
Prachin Buri	E	16
Nong Khai	NE	15
Yaso Thon	NE	12
Trang	S	9
Prachuap Khiri Khan	S	7
Kanchanaburi	W	6
Kampaeng Phet	C	6
Trat	E	6
Krabi	S	5
Nakorn Sawan	C	5
Ang Thong	C	5
Uthai Thani	C	5
Phang-nga	C	2
Suphan Buri	C	1

N: north; NE: northeast; S: south; C: central; E: east; W: west.

ious socioeconomic measures directed at the poor, and an expansion of the self-defense units in the villages. While some of these approaches are not entirely new to Southeast Asia (in Vietnam, Laos, and elsewhere), many observers believed that Prem's leadership and intolerance of corruption would ensure greater effectiveness in the continued implementation of these measures in the rural areas. This seemed to be the case throughout 1982, as rural-based CPM counterinsurgency operations increased with relative success. In early December, more than three thousand CPT members and sympathizers from Operational Zone 444 in Tak province surrendered en masse.[23] Yet urban unrest, particularly in Bangkok, reemerged in 1980 and began to spread throughout 1982 among students and workers due to a renewed attempt by old-line labor leaders to mobilize workers.

NOTES

1. Jean Lacoutre, *Ho Chi Minh* (Paris: Editions de Sevil, 1967).
2. Ibid., p. 41.
3. The Vietnamese had an effective resistance organization under the leadership of Ho Chi Minh, who also collaborated with the OSS.
4. Sarit became particularly well known for his repressive regime, which included such measures as public executions of suspected arsonists and communists. He jailed Kularb Saipradit for his writings, and even had the popular Kukrit Pramoj arrested for criticizing the American ambassador to Thailand in his newspaper, *Siam Rath*. Sarit also gained notoriety for his social life, which included the maintenance of more than 130 wives and mistresses. It was rumored that Sarit enjoyed forcibly seducing Thai beauty contestants while they were fully dressed and he wore only a red Thai sarong (*paka ma daeng*). To avoid confrontation with the feared *paka ma daeng*, beauty contests in Thailand were discontinued until Sarit died.
5. See Melvin Gurtov, *China and Southeast Asia—the Politics of Survival* (Baltimore: Johns Hopkins University Press, 1975), p. 12.
6. Ibid.
7. Ibid.
8. See R. K. McCabe, *Storm Over Asia: China and Southeast Asia, Thrust and Response* (New York: New American Library, 1967), p. 108.
9. *Jen-min-jih-pao*, 17 April 1965, p. 2, in Gurtov, *China and Southeast Asia*, p. 14.
10. Ibid.
11. Ibid., p. 17.
12. Ibid.
13. However, after the Pathet Lao assumed a dominant role in the coalition government of Laos (1971–1974) and the complete takeover by the communist Pathet Lao in 1975, it was generally believed that most of the Thai-Lao had already begun to assist the CPT directly.
14. From a special joint issue of the two monthly magazines, *Ronin* (published in Japan) and *Phuen* (published in Thailand) no. 15, July 1974, p.44.
15. Ibid.
16. Ibid.
17. Ibid.
18. One astute observer of the CPT's efforts at recruitment has pointed out that CPT cadres, when assessing the situation in localities in order to mobilize the masses, "must survey all the social structures of the village and evaluate all changes in order to better reach the people; they must know the attitudes of the people to both the government and insurgents; they must know the history, the

	living conditions, and the economic status of the people. Only after such an exhaustive survey can cadres start to look for suitable recruits and adapt their propaganda to the realities of the particular village situation."
19.	The source of Table 1 is *Com Ti Rak* ("Communist Darling"), a book published in Thai in 1974 by Colonel Han Phongsitanon, Colonel Wichain Songhaprawan, Police Captain Manas Satayarak, Police Major Anand Senakhan, Wirun Tanchareon, Police Captain Varasith Sumon, and Police Sergeant Wichit Sirikun—all officers of the CSOC (Communist Suppression Operations Command). Most of these persons were subsequently indicted for printing, almost verbatim, secret reports of the CSOC.
20.	Ibid.
21.	Table 2 was adapted from figures which appeared in *Bangkok World*, 10 March 1979, p. 3.
22.	After leaving the CPT jungle bases, Thirayuth left for the Netherlands with his wife and child to pursue postgraduate studies, while Seksan began work on a graduate degree in the United States at Cornell University.
23.	*Bangkok Post*, 2 December 1982, p. 1.

3
The Workers

Labor associations in Thailand began as early as 1897 with the establishment of the Association of Tramway Workers and other organizations of workers in the transport, shipping, and rice milling industries.[1] Although few other union groups were established until the 1920s, strong unions were formed among self-employed workers such as motor tricycle drivers and peddlers rather than among wage earners. Several unions were also established in larger factories, but outside Bangkok even factory workers were organized in unions by region rather than by industry and their membership included varied occupations.

Two communist-oriented organizations, the General Labor Union and the Young Workers General Labor Union, were established in 1924 and grew steadily in strength until 1933, when the Thai government enacted anticommunist measures which limited their activities and greatly reduced their membership. Communist-oriented unions were given a temporary reprieve during World War II, however, and the trade unions joined in establishing the Bangkok Federation of Trade Unions in 1944 and in 1945 merged with the communist-dominated Central Labor Union to resist the Japanese. By May 1947, the Central Labor Union had fifty-one member unions. The strongest units were those organized among railroad and streetcar workers, bus drivers, and workers on the waterfront, in rice mills, and in sawmills.

After the war, however, the Thai government attempted to counter the activities of the Central Labor Union. Various ministries either sponsored or financed other labor organizations, such as the Thai

National Trade Union Congress, the Free Workmen's Association of Thailand, and the United Thai Federation of Labor.

The Thai National Trade Union Congress (TNTUC), composed of occupational and regional unions, adopted a constitution in 1951 which supported cooperation between labor and capital. The strongest unions in the TNTUC were the Union of Motor Tricycle Drivers, the peddlers' union, and an organization of small shopkeepers. The TNTUC's membership included employees in government-owned factories and extended to miners, rubber tappers, and plantation workers in the south and to tobacco and teak workers and some farm and plantation laborers in the north.

The Free Workmen's Association of Thailand (FWAT), registered with the government in 1953, was formed in order to draw Chinese workers away from the communist-dominated Central Labor Union. The FWAT received considerable financial support from the director general of the National Police Department and, like the TNTUC, was linked to the political ambitions of Prime Minister Phibun Songkram. According to some sources, Phibun, having observed that all democratic countries had trade unions, decided to allow trade union movements to develop as part of a return to a constitution and elections. It was also at this time that the Phibun government enacted the Labor Law of 1956.

THE LABOR LAW OF 1956

For a society which was principally agrarian, the Labor Law of 1956 was idealistic in many respects. For an economically developing nation, however, the three major divisions—labor protection measures, procedures for establishing a union or federation, and rules governing industrial relations—were practical. Protective measures included prohibition of women under eighteen years of age from engaging in certain types of work, a minimum age for child labor (age twelve), equal pay for equal work regardless of sex, time and a half for overtime, and a maximum 48-hour work week with an 8-hour day (which was in accordance with International Labor Organization standards in effect at that time).

The liberal provisions of the law did not, however, reflect the conservative actions taken by the government. As the trade unions developed, unions in communist countries quite naturally invited labor leaders to visit their countries. Many of the leaders responded to the invitation and went to Moscow and Peking, only to be thrown in jail upon their return to Thailand. These actions of the Phibun government only increased union demands for broader, more general, workers' rights.

Basically there were two substantial deficiencies in the Labor Law. First, there was no provision for a minimum wage. Second, there was no effective method of mediating employer/employee disagreements. Disputes between employers and employees continued to be settled through intervention by local administrators, police, central government ministries, or direct action by the prime minister. Ironically, even with these deficiencies the Labor Law of 1956 was found to be too liberal by the military junta in power at the time, and it was subsequently abrogated in October 1958 by order of Field Marshal Sarit Thanarat. Sarit led a successful coup against the Phibun government, banned the trade union movement completely, and arrested most of its leaders.

Elimination of the Labor Law of 1956 resulted in the termination of all labor organizations. Authority for formulating protective labor legislation was transferred to the minister of interior, who was further charged with the responsibility of settling labor disputes and inspecting labor establishments.[2] Since under Sarit's rule any striker could be jailed, work stoppages due to strikes and lockouts were minimal until 1969.[3]

Although trade unions were effectively banned during Sarit's administration, there were in fact some workers' strikes. In 1962, there were seven short strikes in which demands were limited to better wages, facilities, and conditions. During the six years of Sarit's rule the longest strike, which lasted two months, involved workers at the Firestone Tire Company. Many of the leaders of this strike were jailed for terms ranging from six to eight years. In the aftermath of the student revolution of 1973, by contrast, there were more than a hundred strikes, but none of the leaders were jailed and most of the workers' demands were met.

THANOM AND THE LABOR LAW OF 1971

Thanom Kittikachorn, who replaced Sarit as prime minister, promulgated a new labor law in April 1971, when the country was once again experimenting with democratic institutions after the elections of 1969. The Labor Law of 1971 allowed workers to form employees' associations. It was surmised at the time that Thanom wanted to build support from the labor movement, once legalized, to meet the eventuality of elections in the future. Although it was thought that Thanom would win over workers' votes through these associations, workers were rather suspicious at this sudden change of attitude on the administration's part and only three employee associations were registered at first.

Six months after this labor law was passed, pending labor disputes were once again temporarily "solved" by direct government action. In November 1971, Thanom decided to put the country under martial law and rule by executive decree. It was not surprising, therefore, that the most articulate labor leaders concluded that periodic government-supported labor laws were not the solution to the workers' problems. Instead of laws without adequate implementation, some labor leaders argued that in-country training for workers was essential if the labor movement was to spread.

Snan Vongsuthee, labor leader of the Brotherhood of Asian Trade Unions (BATU), was instrumental in organizing in-country training programs, which included more than four hundred workers from the railroads and the tobacco and textile industries. These training programs included an important educational component to increase the political awareness of the workers and sustain the momentum of the movement. Also discussed in these sessions were strategies of collective bargaining, including strikes, walkouts, and the viability of the student-worker alliance.

Just prior to the October 1973 uprising, various student leaders (Seksan and others) had been in contact with labor leaders and some students even assisted in the development of the political education aspect of the worker training programs. Also during this time it was the students who helped warn various worker movements that the police were planning a complete crackdown on their political activities. The special branch of the police investigation unit, Central Investigation Division (CID), in Bangkok had already begun monitoring the training activities. As one labor leader stated in an interview in 1974, "They [the police] used to follow us to our training sessions and would be waiting for us outside when we finished."

THE STUDENTS' ROLE IN THE WORKER MOVEMENT

Students were a great help to the workers' cause after 1971, but in a 1974 interview the labor leader Snan recalled the October 1973 revolt: "It wasn't all students; whatever they may say, the students didn't drive the buses at the time of the demonstrations and confrontations—workers did!"

The successful collaboration between students and workers became particularly evident about eight months after the October revolt of 1973. During the months of May and June 1974, Bangkok witnessed a series of student-supported strikes. In mid-May, Thailand witnessed its first strike by public school teachers. As noted earlier, one teacher cut his wrist while addressing a crowd of teachers demanding the resignation of Education Minister Abhai.[4] Three days later Abhai resigned and the teachers' demands were met. On 23 May, three hundred Bang Kae Transportation Company bus conductors went on a five-hour strike demanding a pay raise and a paid holiday. One bus conductor was clubbed and stabbed to death while trying to get the conductors to return to work. Thereafter a small group of conductors staged a brief strike stranding hundreds of passengers. Within hours the transportation company yielded to the strikers' demands.

About one week later (4 June 1974), garbage collectors went on strike leaving two hundred garbage trucks standing idle. Workers' demands included a one-year retroactive wage increase, a shift to a permanent public payroll to replace the day-to-day basis of payment, and three months of compensation for the high cost of living.[5]

These strikes were only a slight indication of what was fast becoming a formidable student-worker movement. The organizational ability and political strategy of this new force were particularly evident in the student-supported textile workers' strike.

THE TEXTILE WORKERS' STRIKE

During the first week of June 1974, three Thai student groups—the National Student Center of Thailand (NSCT), the People for Democracy Group (PDG), and the Federation of Independent Students of Thailand (FIST)—began assisting textile workers in their slowdown protest against mill owners. Textile manufacturers had requested government assistance in lowering the tax for raw materials to compensate for the slowdown. When the Thai government rejected their proposal, the textile mill owners laid off 25 percent of the work force. Labor leaders and student groups rallied to the workers' cause and organized three thousand mill workers to force the reinstatement of the laid-off textile workers. The workers went in busloads to the industrial Phra Pradaeng area in an attempt to rally the support of some ten thousand textile workers there. The protesting workers had six demands which included reinstatement of laid-off workers, revision of the labor law, and changing temporary workers to permanent status.

When the workers received no response from the minister of labor, the protesters seized the Labor Department compound for an all-night vigil. Student leaders from Ramkamhaeng University proudly stated to the press that "we are fighting not only for the textile workers but for the benefit and security of workers throughout the country."[6] By 10 June most of the workers' demands were met in principle by the employers. There was still no agreement, however, on a minimum wage increase, changes in compensation clauses in the labor law, and retroactive pay for striking workers.

The momentum of the movement increased at a pace reminiscent of the October revolt, as Thailand's organized labor force, 400,000 strong, represented by the thirty-four workers' associations, decided to unite behind the strikers. Student groups stepped up the pressure as student leaders and other activists continued their speeches denouncing the "blood-sucking foreign capitalists."[7]

In the meantime, striking workers were given a boost when workers from the railway, the plastic factories, and glass factories joined the protest. An effigy representing a Japanese capitalist was hung from a wooden pole during the protest at the Pramain Ground. After six days of labor unrest, the government offered the striking workers an employment plan which, among other things, provided for job security and a compromise minimum-wage increase.

By all indications it became obvious that the workers, supported by the students, had won another victory. Unprecedented labor organization and tactics had produced unprecedented concessions on the part of government and industry. Government and industry leaders soon experienced the implications of this victory for labor in Thailand, as they witnessed a series of prolabor legislation enacted in the two weeks following the strike.

The series of strikes and government responses ushered in a new attitude toward change on the part of the many common Thai laborers. Although the average Thai worker was still basically culture-bound in the sense that his lowly position was perceived as his karma (destiny) for this life, many Thai laborers became aware of the advantages of direct confrontation as a means of change. Workers apparently were no longer completely intimidated by a tradition which demanded strict adherence to one's *naa tii* (duty) in occupational status and place in society vis-à-vis the *phuu yai* (superiors). In a significant departure from previous labor movements in Thailand, workers now demanded rights and privileges in addition to financial benefits. This attitude, adopted by a significant number of the *phuu noi* (common laborers) in Bangkok, contagiously spread to other laborers in Bangkok and the provinces.

A good illustration of the example set by the textile workers' strike is the case of the Hotel Workers' Union, which emerged as a new and significant force in the Thai labor movement. Therdphun Chaidee, a former student of Thammasat University, became a dynamic and charismatic leader of the Hotel Workers' Union, which by June 1975 claimed more than five thousand members in Bangkok.

Moreover, labor leaders and many of their followers sought representation through promotion of their own candidates in the general elections of 1975 and 1976. Protest marches and demonstrations, which became a prevailing mode of political participation during this period (1974–1976), were adopted by even the most unlikely civil service employees. Several incidents involved rank-and-file policemen and soldiers who used slowdowns, strikes, and demonstrations. One such demonstration by soldiers in 1975 culminated in the looting and vandalizing of Prime Minister Kukrit Pramoj's private residence.

Problems of Labor Union Development

While the textile workers' strike was a landmark in the Thai labor movement, and subsequent union activity stimulated union development, serious problems involving continuity and organization continued to plague the movement. Although the prevailing political environment was conducive to labor union activity, there seemed to be, as one labor leader remarked, "more heat than light." Union gains were often paper promises since no agency existed to implement the newly enacted laws. Almost all major labor disputes were settled through government intervention at the cabinet level. The legislature, the courts, and ministries of labor and industry were rarely involved in the process of mediation and arbitration. The labor unions were able to obtain a minimum wage law but were not able to legitimize the process of collective bargaining with management. Their failure was due as much to an inability to organize themselves internally as it was due to management's refusal to recognize the unions as official representatives of their employees. Intermediate union officials between the union president and the employees such as shop stewards, or their equivalent, were almost nonexistent.

Most unions did not provide their members with the customary manual of rules and procedures but instead distributed occasional leaflets describing a particular issue during a strike. Through such pamphlets union leaders sought to make employees aware of their exploitation by management and to explain that they were in a position to get higher wages if they went on strike. Union membership was not required nor were its advantages completely understood by workers. This fact became evident after the author interviewed more than two hundred striking workers from Sony and other factories during the summer of 1975.

Another problem facing the labor movement, generic to most social movements, was the question of cooperation among the various unions. The unity of purpose which marked the success of the textile workers' strike unfortunately followed the very same process of disintegration that faced the NSCT several months after the successful student revolt of October 1973. Unity now gave way to power struggles for leadership positions within unions as well as contention between unions. Disputes between labor leaders ranged from petty personality conflicts to ideological battles over the role of the labor movement. These ideological differences usually involved different approaches to achieve workers' gains, and the Russian versus the American experience was often cited as a model for development of the labor movement.

The gains of the Thai labor movement came to an abrupt halt in the aftermath of the government's bloody battle with students at Thammasat University in October 1976. Worker training sessions and strikes were outlawed, and all forms of union activity became suspect by the new right-wing regime, which sought to attract new investments by appeasing the business sector. Previous labor legislation was superseded by the new regime's right to rule by "executive decree," which included the extended use of Article 21.[8] This article was used to arrest and detain several thousand student, worker, and farmer leaders in the aftermath of the bloody coup of 1976. Many worker leaders went underground; some, such as Therdphun Chaidee, even joined the new front organizations created by the CPT.

The Labor Reform Bill of 1978

In preparation for a return to constitutional rule and elections, and after a series of strikes in 1978, the government established the National Labor Development Advisory Committee, which was fashioned after the U.S. National Labor Relations Board. The new Thai National Legislative Assembly (NLA), the members of which were appointed by the government, passed a 62-article bill that removed labor disputes from the civil and criminal courts and established a separate labor court to settle disputes. The new labor court was to have three judges: one selected by the employer, one by the employee or his representative, and one selected by the government. This bill also provided for the division of the various labor courts into three geographic jurisdictions: a central court for Bangkok and surrounding provinces, regional courts for the north, south, northeast, and so forth, and provincial courts to hear cases in the outlying provinces.

In response to the liberal labor legislation, unions emerged once again and began grouping together in national labor federations. The four main groupings of unions were the National Council of Thai Labor (NCTL), which claimed about sixty member unions, the Labor Congress of Thailand (LCT) with around forty-four member unions, the National Federation of Workers Congress (NFWC) with thirty member unions, and the Nonaligned Unions (NU), which numbered about fifteen at the end of 1978.

Previously established unions resurfaced and new unions emerged, some under leaders who had been arrested or detained by the Thanin government. The Metropolitan Water Works Authority (MWWA), for example, was now headed by Arom Pongpa-ngan, a former detainee in the military takeover of 6 October 1976. By September 1979, sixty unions including the MWWA had joined the Labor Congress of Thailand under the leadership of Paisarn Tawatchainand, a former worker-leader. Snan, former worker-leader during and after the October 1973 revolt, became secretary-general of the newly formed NCTL, which had increased its member unions by the end of 1979.

As part of the new Labor Reform Bill, the government established a Labor Relations Committee which included representatives of the LCT, NFWC, and NCTL. All members of the committee, labor and management, were selected by the minister of interior. The selection process, however, became a problem for the government. Immediately after the formation of the committee, Paisarn, president of the LCT, and representatives of the Nonaligned Unions staged a rally to protest the formation of the Labor Relations Committee and the process of selection. The dispute was resolved with Paisarn now included as a member of the committee.

The National Labor Development Advisory Committee (NLDAC) was also established during this period to assist in labor/management disputes and advise on major labor issues. Since members of this committee were considered leftist-oriented by government officials, however, the role of the NLDAC was minimal.

Workers in various industries began to reemerge with an improved organizational base. The militant protests of hotel workers during the 1973–1976 era, for example, were replaced by the organization of the first Hotel Labor Federation in Thailand. This new union organized all the workers at the Narai, President, Hyatt Rama, and Amarin hotels.

In January 1979, the city's public transportation was paralyzed when most of the twenty-two thousand workers of the Bangkok Mass Transit Authority (BMTA) went on strike to protest the government's delay in adjusting their wages. General Serm ordered the workers back to work "or else"[9] and also met with government officials of the BMTA and Labor Department in an attempt to resolve the conflict. In the meantime Snan, secretary-general of the National Congress of Thai Labor (NCTL), claimed that the one-day strike by bus drivers was incited by "malicious persons attempting to upset the upcoming elections."[10] Snan claimed that right-wing elements—not the NCTL or any other labor organization—were behind the strike in an attempt to convince Prime Minister Kriangsak that due to labor unrest the elections scheduled for April should not be held.[11]

In February 1979, when workers of the foreign-owned Phranakorn

Milk Industry staged a prolonged slowdown over a dispute concerning fringe benefits, management dismissed 101 of the 125 employees. An earlier dispute had gone to the Labor Relations Committee, which handed down a decision in January that supported management's position.

The establishment of the Labor Relations Committee and the rest of the dispute resolution apparatus set up as a result of the 1978 reforms were far-reaching on paper but not quite implemented as planned. By the end of 1979 the lower levels of the dispute resolution system, the three levels of labor courts, had still not been set up to hear cases. Hence newly formed unions remained in constant conflict with management and commonly resorted to slowdowns, strikes, and protest marches.

In July 1979, the first major labor rally since the imposition of martial law drew ten thousand persons including representatives of more than one hundred unions at Sunam Luang, a popular protest site in Bangkok. Throughout 1979, union growth and support in the private and public sectors gained momentum and wildcat strikes once again became the main weapon for unions in pressing for concessions. In the fall of 1979, strikes by government workers of the State Railway of Thailand (SRT), Telephone Organization of Thailand (TOT), and Metropolitan Water Works Authority (MWWA) were eventually joined by eleven other government employees' organizations in demanding higher wages.

In the private sector, more than six thousand longshoremen walked off their jobs in a wage dispute. The strike paralyzed the movement of cargo of thirty-two shipping firms for two days at an estimated cost of 150 million baht. In the end, management conceded to workers' demands of a 15 baht per day raise. In January 1980, a ten-day walkout by the government-owned Thai Tobacco Monopoly caused Prime Minister Kriangsak to cancel a visit to West Germany.

Throughout 1980, strikes among government employees and private-sector workers continued. Slowdowns and work stoppages in critical industries of transportation and energy were particularly disruptive. In February 1981, citywide deliveries of cooking gas and oil supplies were halted when the Summit Oil workers walked off their jobs over a wage dispute.

By the end of 1981 the labor movement, which had played a very active role in Thai politics after 1973, once again began to increase its influence. Now, however, there were two major differences: the absence of student participants in strikes and the union leadership's focus on worker-related issues rather than the broad social and ideological issues which motivated labor activity from 1973 to 1976. This new focus was due in part to the government's lifting of the controversial strike ban and also to the creation of improved methods of dispute resolution through the Labor Reform Bill of 1978. The ultimate success of the new collective bargaining arrangements depended on economic progress in the private sector and the viability of the Thai Parliament as a check on the military's dominance of the Thai government. The catalytic role of the students, whose protest demonstrations included support for a viable Parliament and the workers' movement, particularly during periods of martial law, is described in historical perspective in the next chapter.

NOTES

Sections of this chapter were based on a paper prepared for presentation and discussion at the "Workshop on Democratic Processes in Thailand" as part of the ASPAC Annual Conference, 17–19 June 1977, at Eugene, Oregon.

1. Sukdi Pasuknirunt, "A Comparative Analysis Between the Thai Labor Law and U.S. Labor Legislation" (Ph.D. dissertation, Indiana University, 1959), p. 23.
2. Daniel Wit, *Labor Law and Practice in Thailand* (Washington: U.S. Department of Labor, 1962), p. 33.
3. Department of Labor, Ministry of Interior, *Yearbook of Labor Statistics, 1969* (Bangkok, 1970), pp. 202–230.
4. *Nation*, 19 May 1974.
5. *Bangkok Post*, 5 June 1975.
6. *Bangkok Post*, 10 June 1974.
7. *Bangkok Post*, 11 June 1974, p. 2.
8. Article 21, which has long been a part of martial law in Thailand, allows the police to arrest and jail without trial anyone, at any time, who is suspected of disturbing the peaceful order of the kingdom or is believed to be a threat to the country.
9. *Nation*, 30 January 1979, p. 1.
10. *Nation*, 31 January 1979, p. 1.
11. Ibid.

4
Catalysts of the Transition: The Thai Student Movement

> While it is a student's job to study, there are occasions when his decision to lay aside his books and take up a political banner can make a difference in the political future of his country.[1]

Although university students have become less overtly active since 1970 in most Western countries (France and the United States, for example) and even Asian countries (such as Japan and India), the decade of the seventies witnessed a steady increase in the number and intensity of student demonstrations in Thailand. Furthermore, while the membership and effectiveness of student organizations in most Western and Asian nations decreased considerably from 1970 to 1976, the Thai students became increasingly organized, expanded their membership on a national scale, and were more effective in achieving their demands. Moreover, the effectiveness of Thai student demonstrations persisted and even gained momentum after the imposition of martial law in 1971. This development is remarkable when compared with the fate of student activism in the Philippines where, following the imposition of martial law, effective student organizations and activism were almost nonexistent.

The unusual effectiveness of university student protests during the imposition of martial law in Thailand was due largely to the ability of students to mobilize quickly and sustain their demonstrations for several days. The organizational capability of the student movement was greatly facilitated by the formation of the National Student Center of Thailand in 1969. In fact, its establishment became a turning point in the evolution of the Thai student movement.

ACTIVISM

Thailand, unlike India, lacks any real tradition of student activism. In the early 1900s while Indian students protested political issues (such as the partition of Bengal—1905), Thai university students, few in number in any case, remained detached from political matters, which were left entirely to the king and Royal Council until 1932. The only student activism prior to this time was by Marxist-oriented Chinese university students who had fled China in 1927. In fact, Thai university students as such were nonexistent until 1916, when by royal command the status of the Civil Servants School was elevated to that of a university and named Chulalongkorn University in memory of King Chulalongkorn the Great. It was not until June 1932 that the absolute monarchy was abolished in a bloodless coup and the reins of government were transferred to a military and civilian elite.

The liberal ideals of this new ruling clique were reflected in higher education; in 1933, just one year after the coup, the University of Moral and Political Science was founded. This name was later changed to the University of Moral Science (that is, Thammasat University) in 1952, but the curriculum continued to emphasize the humanities, particularly political science and law. In 1942, the Faculty of Medicine was separated from Chulalongkorn University and became Mahidol University, named after the father of Bhumibhol, the present king of Thailand. In 1943, the School of Agriculture and the School of Forestry were combined to establish the first agricultural institution of higher learning, Kasetsart University. Silapakorn University, specializing primarily in architecture and the fine arts, was founded in the same year. In 1954, the College of Education was established and granted university status; its prime objectives are to train teachers, school administrators, and educational research workers. Since its conception, various other educational programs have been added, and the College of Education now comprises several campuses in Bangkok with other campuses spread throughout the outer provinces of Thailand.

These five universities, though all institutions of higher learning, were not all administered by the Ministry of Education. Only Chulalongkorn, Thammasat, and Silapakorn universities were under the jurisdiction of the Ministry of Education; Kasetsart University was administered by the Ministry of Agriculture and Mahidol University by the Ministry of Public Health. In 1959, however, all five universities were placed under the Prime Minister's Office and in 1963, as a result of the Prime Minister's Office Organization Act, each university gained the legal status of a ministry department. Soon thereafter the National Council of Educa-

Table 3
Enrollment, Year of Foundation, and Location of Thai Universities

Name of University	Enrollment in 1972	Year of Foundation	Location
Chulalongkorn	12,450	1916	Bangkok
Thammasat	9,148	1933	Bangkok
Mahidol	3,901	1942	Bangkok
Kasetsart	6,007	1943	Bangkok
	262	1943	Bangkok
Silapakorn College of Education	15,979	1954	Bangkok (three campuses) and provinces (five campuses)
Chiang Mai	7,236	1964	Chiang Mai
Khonkaen	1,649	1964	Khonkaen
Songkla Nakarin	788	1967	Songkla and Pattani
Ramkamhaeng	28,611	1971	Bangkok
Total	86,031		

Source: Office of the National Education Council.

tion was established as a coordinating committee whose primary concerns are the activities of all universities.

Of these five universities, only Chulalongkorn maintained a broad curriculum offering degrees in several areas of study. Kasetsart University offered courses only in agriculture; Mahidol provided instruction only in medicine, Thammasat University in jurisprudence, and Silapakorn in various areas of art. Since 1965, however, each of these universities has expanded the scope of its curriculum, particularly in the humanities. Moreover, several more recently established universities offer a broad base of academic fields of study and provide educational opportunities to the residents of outer provinces. In 1964, Chiang Mai University was established in the northern capital of Chiang Mai province; in the same year Khonkaen University was created to afford higher educational opportunities to the residents of the northeastern provinces of Thailand. In 1967, the University of Songkla Nakarin was opened to residents of southern Thailand; eventually it included a Faculty of Education at Pattani and also a campus at Haadyai specializing in engineering and medical sciences.

Before the establishment of these universities in the provinces, Bangkok was, and to a large extent still remains, the primary residence of university students; in fact, the universities in Bangkok still provide more than 90 percent of the country's graduates.[2] This percentage was somewhat increased with the establishment of Ramkamhaeng University in 1971. Located in Bangkok and named in memory of the famous king of the Sokuthai era, this university was created through the efforts of liberal Parliament members only months before martial law was declared in 1971. Beginning with primarily a liberal arts curriculum and an open admissions policy, Ramkamhaeng has had to adjust and expand its programs to the demands of an ever-increasing rate of enrollment. Enrollment figures, founding dates, and locations of the Thai universities are shown in Table 3.

LOCATION OF UNIVERSITIES IN BANGKOK

Since university students' protest marches always take place in Bangkok, the locations of the universities in Bangkok are of prime importance if one is to understand student activism in Thailand. Thammasat University may be used as the starting point to visualize the geographical implications of student activism. Thammasat University is located near the Old Palace where all kings of Bangkok preceding Rama V have resided.[3] Silapakorn University lies between Thammasat and the palace.

In front of these two universities there is a large open field called Pramain Ground. In ancient times it served as the cremation site for members of the royal family. It is now used for the New Year's Day Festival, the Water Festival, the Ploughing Ceremony, kite fighting, and an open market where goods from the provinces are sold each weekend. On one side of Pramain Ground there begins one of the widest, and most beautiful, streets of Bangkok: Rajdamnern Avenue. Located on the other end of this avenue is the Parliament Building with the office of the prime minister nearby. Along this avenue, about one kilometer from Pramain Ground, lies the Democracy Monument erected by the 1932 revolutionaries. Protest marches by the students almost always start from Pramain Ground and move along Rajdamnern Avenue to the Parliament Building or the office of the prime minister. Being both wide and not very long, this avenue is ideal in accommodating the huge throngs of students who participate in the protest marches.

Chulalongkorn University is about eight kilometers southeast of Pramain Ground. The main campus of the College of Education is about fourteen kilometers east of Pramain Ground, while Mahidol University is located only about one-half kilometer from the Parliament Building. Kasetsart University is somewhat farther from this site, located about twenty kilometers north of the Parliament Building.

The map in Figure 1 depicts the approximate locations of the various

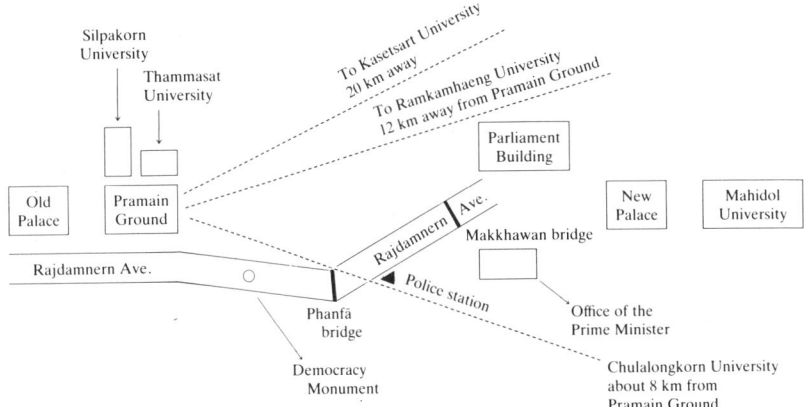

Figure 1   Location of universities in Bangkok

universities and their relative proximity to Pramain Ground and to each other. As one can imagine, the location of the universities has significant implications not only for the strategy of the student protests but also for government attempts to stop them. The openness of the area of Rajdamnern Avenue lends itself to tempered responses by government officials, who hesitate to display force in an arena-like atmosphere. All the major student demonstrations described below followed the path to Pramain Ground before pressing demands directly on the government administrators.

Major Student Demonstrations

Anti-French Demonstration of 1940

The first incidence of student activism occurred in November 1940. The roots of that demonstration can be traced back almost forty years earlier when Thailand was forced to cede sections of its eastern territory to France in 1903 and 1910.[4] The Thais had always desired to reclaim this territory. When war broke out in Europe in 1939, the Thai government declared Thailand to be a neutral state; but when France surrendered in June 1940, the Thai government seized the opportunity to regain the lost territory and staged an extensive anti-French propaganda campaign. In November 1940, there were anti-French demonstrations by Thais throughout the country.[5] Chulalongkorn and Thammasat university students joined these demonstrations, which were being promoted by various organizations in Bangkok.

Thammasat Students vs. the Army

After World War II, the reins of government were briefly in the hands of Pridi Panomyong, one of the most powerful and respected civilian leaders. As leader of the Free Thai Movement, a volunteer underground army which opposed Japanese occupation, Pridi claimed a great following among the civilian population. As one of the 1932 revolutionaries, he was also the founder of Thammasat University and an instructor there.[6] In November 1947, a military coup forced him to leave the country and his followers, most of them civilians who had graduated from Thammasat University, were driven out of politics.[7]

With a group of his most loyal followers, Pridi attempted a coup in February 1949. Supported by some navy men and several civilian leaders, many of whom used to be his students, he slipped into Thammasat University one night and held a meeting among his followers in one of the campus buildings. Many of the university lecturers and administrators were old students and admirers of his. After the meeting, Pridi and his followers went on to seize the Old Palace nearby. Some of his men took over the government radio station and announced the news of the coup. Within two days, however, Pridi's forces were crushed by the army and Pridi had to flee the country again.[8] Although many university administrators were detained for questioning, there was little effect on Thammasat University students at the time. Even after the army took over part of the main campus and occupied it, students continued to study in other parts of the campus.

In June 1959, there was another bloody coup led by a group of navy men. During the fight some of the ground troops occupied the Thammasat campus to fortify their position in combating the rebellion nearby. A few days after its beginning the rebellion was crushed by government forces. The army remained at Thammasat University, however, claiming that the campus was located in a strategic area. Moreover, the government claimed that since the campus had been used by the army in the coup of 1949, they were justified in their occupation of the campus. Thammasat University was then closed for about a month.

In late August 1959, some Thammasat students were directed to attend Chulalongkorn University while others were told to study at the auditorium of the Ministry of Justice. Thammasat students at that time wanted to come back to Thammasat, but they were confused as to what course of action, if any, they should take. About two months later, and after much debate, the students decided to do something about the situation. On 11 October about two thousand students attended a session of Parliament and asked one of the M.P.'s to request the government to withdraw its troops from Thammasat University. The government representatives replied that it was necessary for the army to occupy this "strategic area" in order to maintain law and order; they refused to specify when the government would withdraw its troops. At the end of the session the students asked to see the prime minister, Field Marshal Phibun Songkram. It should be pointed out that Phibun Songkram was once a friend of Pridi Panomyong, the founder of Thammasat University, but later they became archrivals. The students avoided ridiculing Phibun for what he had done; instead they praised him in unison: "Long live Field Marshal Phibun Songkram". Then they asked him to withdraw the troops from the campus.[9] Phibun assured the students that the troops would move out, but he did not give a specific date. In November about three thousand Thammasat students traveled to Nakornsawan, a northern town about 250 kilometers from Bangkok, and returned to Bangkok on 5 November 1951. Then, instead of going home, they went together in buses to Thammasat University. They marched on the campus and walked in to "inspect" the buildings. The soldiers were quite unprepared to receive the unarmed though apparently angry students. After a few hours of badgering the soldiers and asking them why they were occupying the university, the students left peacefully. A few days later the government withdrew its troops from the campus, and Thammasat University was reopened to the students again.[10] It was rumored with some evidence at this time that the government had specific plans for closing the university permanently, regarding it as an undesirable stronghold for Pridi Panomyong and his followers. It was pressure from the students that finally obliged the government to abandon this plan.

Protesting the "Dirty Election" of 1957

In February 1957, a general election was held throughout the country. Field Marshal Phibun Songkram and eight members of his party were candidates for the Bangkok seats. After the results were in, there was evidence to suggest that Phibun's followers had used unfair tactics to get the candidates of Phibun's party elected.[11] Public dissatisfaction with the conduct of the election in February 1957—dissatisfaction which was vigorously expressed in the press and among students—caused the government to declare a national emergency. This move only fanned the flames of anger among the civilian population of Bangkok, however, and they began to gather regularly at Pramain Ground. They were joined there by increasing numbers of students from Chulalongkorn and Thammasat universities to criticize the government publicly for the allegedly fraudulent election. In the meantime, students on the Chulalongkorn University campus displayed protest signs accusing Phibun of destroying democracy.[12]

Several days later, the Chulalongkorn students marched from their campus to join with the people and students of other universities at Pramain Ground. They then marched to the office of the prime minister, breaking through police barriers along the way. Although the police attempted to force the demonstrators to stop the march without using guns, many eyewitness reports indicated that when the marchers were asked to stop at the bridge near the office of the prime minister, the soldiers and police were about to open fire. Only at the last moment did the police officer in charge finally order his men to let the demonstrators pass without incident. This incident marked the only time that confrontation with police led to the brink of violence. This remained the situation throughout all future Thai demonstrations up until the violent overthrow of the Thanom government in October 1973.

When the protesters finally got to the government building housing the office of the prime minister, they broke down the gate and forced themselves inside demanding to meet with Phibun. The prime minister eventually came out, spoke to the protesters, and promised to remedy the situation. The person most responsible for calming the still hostile student demonstrators, however, was Field Marshal Sarit Thanarat. Later, in September 1957, Sarit, riding the tide of widespread opposition among the Bangkok populace and with tacit student support, led a coup against the Phibun government and drove him and his most powerful allies out of the country.

University students were not the only demonstrators in this protest, it should be noted. The general population of Bangkok, including workers, professionals, and politicians, all took part in the massive protest movement against the Phibun government for its handling of the election and the subsequent declaration of a "national emergency."

Demonstration Against the World Court

In October 1958, Sarit carried out another bloodless coup and declared himself prime minister. He abrogated the constitution, proclaimed martial law, and appointed a committee to draft a new constitution. Martial law remained in effect until 1968 when the new constitution was completed. During this ten-year period under martial law there was a major demonstration against the World Court.

In 1959, Kampuchea requested the World Court to rule on the withdrawal of Thai police forces from the temple grounds of Khao Praviharn, an ancient temple on the border of Thailand and Kampuchea, which they had occupied since 1954. The case remained unresolved with the World Court for four years until 15 June 1962, when the court ruled in favor of Kampuchea. This decision ignited demonstrations throughout Thailand. University students did not initiate the demonstrations, but after a few days of general public protest in Bangkok and other cities they joined in one of the largest student demonstrations ever to be staged in Thailand up to that time.

On 21 June 1962, more than fifty thousand students marched from Pramain Ground to the Parliament Building shouting slogans and carrying placards denouncing the World Court's verdict. The students represented all the major universities of Bangkok including Chulalongkorn, Thammasat, Mahidol, Silapakorn, and Kasetsart.[13] In front of the Parliament Building, hundreds of students of the various universities took turns making speeches denouncing both the World Court's verdict and Kampuchea's leaders. Since the government's position on this issue was similar to their own, the students met with little official opposition. In fact, some of the public demonstrations were not only supported by the government but also promoted by government-backed politicians.

Demonstrations Against Martial Law and Higher Bus Fares

The drafting of the new constitution, which began in 1958, was completed in 1968. During this ten-year span Thailand remained under martial law as it was declared and set forth by Sarit in 1958. Although the constitution provided for such civil liberties as freedom of speech and assembly, the Thai government still retained martial law in Bangkok and other parts of the country claiming that it was necessary in order to "protect the national security." The constitution provided for an election to be held within 240 days of the date the constitution went into effect. Thammasat students together with the public and some politicians began requesting that the government lift martial law to ensure a fair election and to show good faith in supporting the constitutional provisions for certain civil liberties which were now being denied. When the students organized and marched from Pramain Ground to the Parliament Building to press for the adoption of their proposals, the government responded by declaring that even though the 1968 constitution had been promulgated, the population of Thailand was still under a law which prohibited public assembly without government approval. Although this demonstration was relatively small it could have been ruled an act of illegal assembly by the government. Rather than engage in an unpopular confrontation just before the election, however, the government complied with the demand of the demonstrators and lifted martial law in Bangkok but retained it in the "threatened areas" of the outer provinces.[14]

In February 1969, immediately following the general election, there was a student demonstration against the raising of bus fares. Thai students rely almost exclusively on the bus system for transportation to and from the university. When the government-supported and operated bus companies raised bus fares 30 percent, many students felt this undue financial hardship to be directed at them for their agitation before the election. Hence a well-organized protest demonstration was directed toward the government to lower the bus fare back to its original price. Instead of confronting the students over what was considered a rather minor issue by top government officials, the prime minister ordered the bus fare lowered to its original price. Soon after this successful demonstration, student representatives from Thammasat, Chulalongkorn, and Chiang Mai universities, and later other universities, formed the National Student Center of Thailand (NSCT). The NSCT was to play a growing role in all the major movements by Thai students up through the student revolution which overthrew the military government in 1973.

Demonstration Against Corruption in Chulalongkorn University

Of all the Thai universities, Chulalongkorn has the largest campus—and as the metropolitan area of Bangkok continues to expand, the land value of Chulalongkorn continues to increase accordingly. One of its holdings, rented to a private firm, was later developed into a huge shopping center in the late 1960s. When the contract for the construction of the shopping center expired, it was rumored that university administrators were bribed while negotiating a new lease with the construction company. Moreover, it became evident that the university received much less money than it should have obtained from the firm. On 8 September 1970, the students held a rally on the campus and demanded to see the deputy director and secretary-general of the university, but both administrators refused to appear. Thereafter students marched to the office of the prime minister and were joined along the way by students from other universities. As they marched, some of the demonstrators stopped to talk to onlookers and explained that "there is a case of corruption at Chulalongkorn University. If not suppressed it will mean disaster for Chulalongkorn and other universities in the future."[15]

At the office of the prime minister ten student representatives went to meet with Thanom and requested that he fire the three university administrators involved in corruption. The students were specifically seeking the removal of the deputy director, the secretary-general, and the dean of architecture. If these three corrupt individuals were not fired, the students said, they would resort to violent means to rid the university of them. The students alleged that these three took part in a dishonest deal from which they gained great personal profit with an overall loss to the university. Thanom assured the students that he would talk to these administrators about the charges, and also discuss the issue with students in the university auditorium.

The following morning the students began another march to the office of the prime minister. After meeting with other members of the National Student Center of Thailand, the students decided that Thanom should take a much stronger stand against the three administrators; a discussion with students in the auditorium would not be sufficient. Again the students demanded to see Thanom, but this time the prime minister refused to meet with them. The students then marched to the Parliament Building nearby, forced their way in, and sat in the places reserved for members of Parliament, vowing that they would not leave until they received a definite answer from the prime minister on the dismissal of the three administrators. Finally Thanom came to see them and explained that he had talked to the authorities of Chulalongkorn University the previous evening until 1:00 A.M. and had then called an urgent meeting of the University Council to consider the matter. He further explained that the council had made two important decisions: First, a special committee would be set up to investigate the allegations of corruption; second, the three persons would be removed from their administrative positions but would remain on the university staff with professor status. Furthermore, Thanom explained that the three could not be fired until there was conclusive evidence of their guilt; legally, their case was still pending. The students expressed satisfaction with the results of the University Council meeting and finally abandoned the Parliament Building and their protest.

From this point onward, all major demonstrations would involve the National Student Center of Thailand, a newly formed student organization with nationwide membership. The formation and growth of this student organization was to become one of the most significant developments in Thai student activism.

Foundation of the NSCT

Before the founding of the National Student Center, students at most Thai universities were organized through student unions. Although strong student unions at each university were usually well organized for such social functions as cheering at university soccer matches, they were characteristically nonpolitical and, for the most part, not linked with other universities. It was not until 1969 that student union leaders from the various universities began cooperating on social and political issues. The first occasion for interuniversity cooperation was the national elections of 1969, when students of all the universities organized informally to supervise the voting at polling places in Bangkok. Ostensibly students were to assure an honest election and prevent the many irregularities which had occurred in the national election of 1957.

After the national election of 1969, a meeting of a student organization called the World University Service was planned for in Chiang Mai. Representatives of all Thai universities attended this meeting and jointly proposed that Thai students should have an interuniversity organization. This assembly was followed by meetings at Kampansan district (Nakonpathom), at Kasetsart University in August 1969, at Chulalongkorn University in September 1969, and at Prasammitra Teachers College in December 1969. A resolution at the last meeting called for students of all undergraduate institutions to organize a student center which became known as the National Student Center of Thailand (NSCT). A committee to draft the constitution for this organization was also appointed at this meeting. There would be two members from each of the eleven institutions: Chulalongkorn University, Thammasat University, Kasetsart University, Silapakorn University, Mahidol University, Chiang Mai University, Khonkaen University, Songkla University, Prasammitra Teachers College, Bangsaen Teachers College, and Patumwan Teachers College.

The constitutional drafting committee set up the following goals for the NSCT:

1. To promote a good relationship among the students of all Thai universities and between Thai students and those of other countries
2. To serve and promote the welfare of the students
3. To promote the students' freedom and to protect their benefits
4. To further educational standards and academic cooperation
5. To promote understanding between students and the people
6. To preserve and promote Thai culture
7. To render services for the welfare of society

Although the constitutional drafting committee began its work in 1970, the final document was not disclosed to the public until February 1973. It provided for the separation of functions and responsibilities described in the following paragraphs.

The NSCT's organization has three main executive organs: the Executive Committee, the Secretariat Committee, and the Financial Committee. Figure 2 indicates the organizational arrangement of the NSCT. The Executive Committee consisted of the chairmen and women of the student unions of every university. The main duties of the Executive

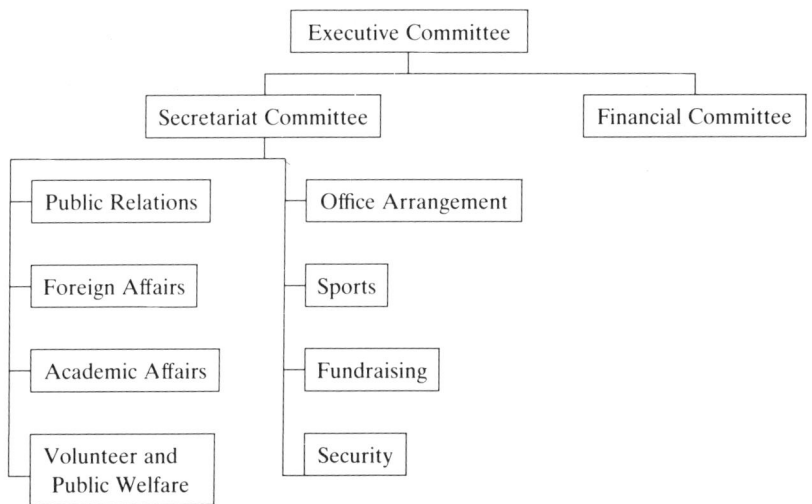

Figure 2   Structure of the NSCT

Committee were twofold: to formulate policy for the NSCT and to select the leaders of all units working under the Secretariat Committee. The Secretariat Committee consisted of one secretary-general and three deputies, all of whom were directly responsible to the Executive Committee. The Secretariat Committee acted as the spokesman of all the universities' leaders. There were functionally oriented subcommittees under the Secretariat Committee: public relations, foreign affairs, academic affairs, volunteer and public welfare, office arrangement, sports, fundraising, and security. The Financial Committee took care of the financial affairs of the center and consisted of a representative from each university. This committee was directly responsible to the Executive Committee.

The secretary-general was the most powerful person in the organizational hierarchy and was ultimately responsible for all NSCT activities. The first secretary-general was chosen from Thammasat University in 1969, as was the second for the academic year 1970–1971. During this period, the NSCT did very little concerning political matters and concentrated its efforts on such social services as fundraising for flood victims, organizing a television program blessing the king, and providing various counseling services to graduating high school students.

For the academic years 1971–1972 and 1972–1973, Thirayuth Boonmee, an engineering student at Chulalongkorn University, was elected secretary-general. Thirayuth was a brilliant student. He not only graduated at the top of his class from one of Thailand's most famous and oldest high schools, Suankularb, but also achieved the highest score of all high school graduates in Thailand on the nationwide university entrance examination. It was under Thirayuth's leadership that the activities of the National Student Center of Thailand turned toward major political issues. Thirayuth started the NSCT on its path toward national recognition and political orientation with a nationwide campaign against Japanese goods in November 1972.

Demonstrations After the 1971 Coup

Before the government elected in 1969 had completed its term of office, the military carried out a successful coup. In November 1971, Thanom Kittikachorn overthrew his own government and subsequently dissolved Parliament, abrogated the 1968 constitution, and declared martial law. Thereafter he formed a government ruled by the National Executive Council and proclaimed himself its leader.

The Campaign Against Japanese Goods

The first incidence of student activism after the 1971 declaration of martial law occurred about a year later in November 1972. For more than ten years Thailand had faced a deficit in the balance of trade with Japan—a deficit that was increasing at an alarming rate for the fiscal years of 1970, 1971, and 1972. By the end of 1972, the trade deficit with Japan was placed at approximately $215 million.[16] In November 1972, the students started a campaign against the purchase of Japanese goods by distributing leaflets to the public. Student leaders then proclaimed 20 to 30 November as "Anti-Japanese Goods Week." During this period they requested the cooperation of the public in refraining from buying Japanese products. The students of various universities acted together under the name of the National Student Center of Thailand. The following translated passage represents parts of the text of the leaflet that was prepared and distributed by the National Student Center:

> Dear Thai Citizen,
> We, the students, who are also your children, are cooperating with one another to refrain from buying Japanese products during "Anti-Japanese Goods Week." The reason for this is that Japan is taking advantage of us by using various business ploys to cheat us and also because the trade dominance by the Japanese in Thailand has increased alarmingly during the past ten years, putting Thailand gradually into a position of Japan's economic slave.

What we are stating here is not far from reality. If you study the actions of Japan or look around and see Japanese dominance in trade and cultural spheres, you will see that what we say is true.

We would not be in trouble at all if the Japanese role was to help to develop our country's economy as they often claim.

If you look at the numerous Japanese goods which have glutted Thai markets and become a part of the everyday life of the Thais, and the influence of advertising (created by Japanese firms), you will realize that a large number of these products are not essential at all. Furthermore, they will cause more damage to the national economy.

We do not want violence because we realize the need for international relations. But if robbers come to our house we have to fight them seriously until they flee or change their behavior.

This movement may be only an insignificant starting point, but it needs cooperation from every sector of the population as it is a fight for righteousness and national progress.

The National Student Center of Thailand, therefore, has asked you to sacrifice your happiness and conveniences, and to save the money you might spend on buying and using Japanese goods and services during Anti-Japanese Goods Week, 20 to 30 November, to show that Thai blood runs thick and cannot be dishonored by anyone.

National Student Center of Thailand
16 November 1972[17]

The students also proposed a ten-point plan for economic revival and presented it to the government on 20 November 1972.[18] Among the major points were the following proposals:

1. The government should urgently enforce laws preventing aliens from taking jobs away from local residents.
2. The foreign-owned department stores are not necessary to the country and the National Executive Council should prohibit the expansion of existing stores and the establishment of new ones.
3. The government should consider controlling or prohibiting the importation of unnecessary goods and investments.

Even though martial law was in existence, the prime minister did not attempt to stop this student movement. He did, however, warn the students that "there must be no violence, not even demonstrations outside the Japanese embassy."[19] Thanom and the deputy prime minister, General Prapas, unofficially expressed admiration for this peaceful student movement against the unpopular Japanese by remarking at one point that the demonstration was a "masterpiece."[20] King Bhumibhol said that the idea of the movement was "excellent" and should receive support because purchases of luxury goods needed to be reduced. However, the king also stated that "careful considerations must be given to what demands are made or the goals of the movement might be defeated."[21]

The movement received general support from the public, and the sale of Japanese goods was greatly reduced during that week. Moreover, in the midst of Anti-Japanese Goods Week the government issued a decree designed to control and protect the Thai economy against Japanese products and investments. The text of the government decree reflected most of the concerns which were stated in the ten-point plan prepared by the National Student Center.

On the last day of Anti-Japanese Goods Week, the students organized a protest march from Pramain Ground to the headquarters of the National Executive Council.[22] Chulalongkorn students tried to go by bus to Pramain Ground, but the police stopped the drivers and ordered them not to transport the students. The students then had to walk to meet fellow students from other universities who had marched from Pramain Ground to the NEC headquarters. When they attempted to get inside the building to see the prime minister, they were stopped by police and security guards. Reporters at the scene of the demonstration gave the following account: "Thousands of shouting students carried their Anti-Japanese Goods protest to the gates of the National Executive Council headquarters last night, but were prevented from forcing their way in by reinforced police and security teams."[23]

Student leaders calmed the demonstrators who at many points nearly clashed with police and security guards. The prime minister did not come out to meet all the students but did send representatives to talk with six student representatives. The prime minister's representatives told the students that Thanom supported them and would attempt to enforce feasible sections of the ten-point plan presented to the government one week earlier.

Demonstration Against Executive Control of the Judiciary

On 12 December 1972 the National Executive Council issued Decree 299, which in effect gave the power to control the nation's judges to the minister of justice, a political appointee of the prime minister. According to the Justice Act of 1952, it was the chief justice of the Supreme Court who held the highest position in the judicial system, presided over all judges in Thailand, and also served as chairman of the Official Judiciary Committee. Decree 299, however, was designed to transfer the chairmanship of this committee to the minister of justice. In addition to assuming all the duties of this chairmanship, the minister of justice, who was directly responsible to the prime minister, was also given expansive power including the power to retire any judge to another ministry if the judge in question agreed to the transfer.

The law students of Thammasat University were quickly made aware of the political implications of Decree 299 as it applied both to their own career goals and to the future of the Thai judicial system. The very next day the law students began a protest movement against the decree. On 15 December 1972, the law students, joined by about two thousand students of other faculties of Thammasat, marched from their campus to Chulalongkorn University. They carried signs, banners, and placards proclaiming such ideals and demands as "Give us back the court," "Dedicated to judiciary power," and "Justice supports the world."[24] Student representatives at Chulalongkorn agreed to support the protest movement and the demands of the Thammasat law students. Soon thereafter, representatives from other universities declared their support for the movement, and on 17 December representatives from all the universities except Songkla presented a letter to the prime minister urging him to retract Decree 299 and order a continuance of the Justice Act of 1952. On the evening of 19 December, thousands of students began a protest rally and a sit-in at Pramain Ground. They remained at this popular protest site throughout the evening and did not disperse until 8:00 A.M. the following day. In the meantime students at the largest and most prestigious university in the provinces, Chiang Mai University, held a protest rally on their campus with students giving speeches denouncing Decree 299.

Almost simultaneously the newly formed cabinet met hurriedly and came to a unanimous decision retracting Decree 299. At 2:27 P.M. the national Thai radio station broadcast the news that the government was going to attempt to approach the demonstrators at the sit-in protest that evening. One cabinet official personally carried the decision and a special message to Thammasat students who were planning to return to the sit-in. Nevertheless, the students decided to go on with the second stage of the sit-in as planned. Aware that the newly appointed Legislative Council had the final authority in the matter, the students wanted decisive action, not promises from government officials. On 22 December, the Legislative Council convened for the first time and Decree 299 was placed at the top of the agenda. Before its first recess of the day the council voted to retract Decree 299 and reenact the Justice Act of 1952.

Demonstration at Ramkamhaeng University

Although Ramkamhaeng University was the last major university to be founded in Thailand, it has the largest enrollment (see Table 3). For Ramkamhaeng, unlike all the other major universities, does not require students to take an entrance examination; rather, it is obliged to consider any student with a high school diploma for admission. Ramkamhaeng University was established not only to educate the many students who failed the entrance examinations of other universities but also to meet one of the primary goals of the five-year plan for higher education; to make a college education available to all who had met the minimum requirements. Because of its limited facilities and enormous enrollment, Ramkamhaeng University allowed and even encouraged students to study at home, and classroom attendance was generally not required. Many students came to the university only at the end of the semester to take their final examinations. Such liberal policies on admissions and attendance do not exist in the other established universities.

The setting for one of the largest protests in the history of Thai student activism began in June 1973, when nine students were expelled from Ramkamhaeng University by order of the rector, Dr. Sakdi Phasooknirand. These students were accused of issuing an illegal magazine attacking the government and personally criticizing the prime minister and deputy prime minister by depicting them as "beasts" in the cartoons and editorials. When classes commenced during the first semester on 20 June 1973, students began to distribute leaflets decrying the expulsion of the "Ramkamhaeng Nine."[25]

In one incident, as students were distributing leaflets at the gate of the university campus, men drove up in a car and began beating them. Other students in the immediate vicinity rushed to the aid of the students being assaulted and in the melee that followed, one of the attackers pulled out a gun and forced the students to retreat while he and his fellow assailants fled in a waiting car.

The following day ten busloads of Ramkamhaeng students were on their way to Chulalongkorn to gather support for their cause, when the buses were stopped by the police and the drivers forced to relinquish their licenses. The government's tactic merely provided an impetus to the movement, however, for the Chulalongkorn students joined the protest and, after meeting with the stranded Ramkamhaeng students, marched together to the Ministry of Government Universities and demanded to see the minister, Dr. Bunpod Bintason. The minister refused to meet with the throngs of students whose number had grown to an estimated ten thousand strong. The students then changed their strategy and decided to congregate at the traditional rallying point: Pramain Ground.

Upon their arrival at Pramain Ground they were greeted by hundreds of students and onlookers. The students then held a huge protest rally with speeches from various student leaders and thereafter proceeded to march to the Democracy Monument. As they advanced they sang a marching song written by some of the students. The lyrics reflected their determination and idealism: "Fight without retreat, for the masses are waiting for us.... We have joined together to fight for democracy!" The students' placards and huge banners expressed the immediacy of the crisis at hand. The banners proclaimed to the onlookers that "Absolutism is taking over higher education" and that "Ramkamhaeng is hot with power" and asked the general population to "Help us escape this danger." On the same day, the official student organization of Chiang Mai University, the Student Front, threw its support behind the student protesters in Bangkok through a communique.

A group of lecturers from various Bangkok universities issued an open letter protesting Ramkamhaeng's dismissal of the nine students. This letter was signed by eighty-two professors, later referred to as "Young Turks," from Chulalongkorn, Thammasat, Silapakorn, Kasetsart, and the National Institute of Development Administration (NIDA).

At the Democracy Monument, the students staged a protest rally and heard speeches from various leaders. The topics of the speeches were not confined only to the case of the nine students at Ramkamhaeng. The students addressed the many problems caused by "power and profit mongers" in high government positions. They called for a new constitution to replace the one that had been abrogated through a military coup in 1971, an end to corruption, and measures to deal with the increasing price of rice and the sagging Thai economy. Determined to remain, the students camped near the monument overnight. Late the same evening, the government ordered the closing of all major universities in Bangkok, including Kasetsart, Chulalongkorn, Thammasat, Mahidol, Ramkamhaeng, Silapakorn, and Prasammitra. The order carried with it a penalty of arrest for any student who tried to enter any campus of these universities. Simultaneously, the government sent about five hundred metropolitan police of the Crime Suppression Division to surround the student camp-in. This "commando" police force proceeded to form a human barricade blocking all routes leading to the Democracy Monument (see Figure 1). The students sought support from the general civilian population by distributing leaflets to publicize their dilemma. The following excerpt is taken from one of the leaflets (translated from Thai):

> To fathers, mothers, and fellow citizens... Now these incidents have indicated that we are ruled by tyrants. They oppress us. They want us to starve because rice is so expensive. No one up there paid any attention to our distress. Our peaceful begging for help did not mean anything to them. Last night students all over the country joined this movement in peace to ask for the rights and freedom which belong to all humanity. We were hungry and cold, but we stayed here until morning. However, the

police surrounded us. They are now saying that they will let your children starve and walk voluntarily up to the barrels of their guns.[26]

The government's move to close the universities proved to be a great mistake. With the universities closed, many students who would have gone to class decided instead to join the sit-in at the Democracy Monument. Kasetsart and Thammasat students came in groups to the scene of the rally. About four thousand Kasetsart students, thwarted by police when attempting to take the bus, walked some twenty kilometers to the Democracy Monument. Before leaving the area around the campus these students held a short rally by the National Museum. Several thousand Thammasat students were the first group to arrive. The police, who had joined to form a human barricade around the Democracy Monument, almost clashed with the arriving throngs of students. After minor skirmishes of pushing and shoving along the barricade line, however, the police finally decided that they had no choice but to allow the thousands of arriving students to go through the line and join the other protesters peacefully.

After the arrival of Kasetsart students the number of the protesters swelled to around thirty thousand,[27] and by midday the figure was placed at about fifty thousand.[28] Almost as impressive as the unity of support by students of all the major universities was the favorable response of the civilian population, who donated money, food, and drink to the protesters throughout their campaign. One report of the incident noted:

> During the long hours of protest, a large amount of food, drink, and money was donated from sympathetic citizens from all walks of life, ranging from street vendors to well-known personalities.... The amount of money collected was more than 40,000 baht [about $2,000].[29]

Periodically during the protest the demonstrators would turn, face the palace, and sing the King's Song, as if to emphasize that even though they were hostile to the government, they still respected the king.

In the meantime, the government attempted to deal with the expanding dimensions of the protest. The cabinet members held an urgent meeting on the morning of 24 June to discuss the matter. After long debate the cabinet members invited the representatives of the students, including the nine expelled students, to see the prime minister and other high officials. As a result of the meeting, the government agreed to the following points:

1. The case of the nine students who were expelled from Ramkamhaeng University would be reconsidered by the Council of Universities.

2. The students' demand for the removal of the rector of Ramkamhaeng University would be reviewed and taken under consideration by the government.
3. The persons who assaulted the students distributing leaflets on the first day of the campaign would be tried and the matter would be taken up by the police department.
4. The government would declare the reopening of all closed universities, and all restrictions pertaining to the shutdown would be retracted.

After the meeting the student leaders reported back to the waiting protesters, explaining that the government, while not conceding to all the demands, did agree to most of what the students wanted. Thereafter the leaders advised the students to disperse and go home.

The next morning, however, the rector of Ramkamhaeng University announced his decision to change the expulsion of the nine students to suspension for one semester.[30] Moreover, one of the nine students, who had been reprimanded by the university administration before this incident, was to be suspended for two semesters. The student leaders who had called an end to the protest demonstration did so with an understanding from the prime minister that the Ramkamhaeng Nine would most likely be readmitted without conditions. The rector's decision to punish the students with suspension succeeded only in angering the student leaders, who thought the crucial issues to be freedom of the press and the right of students to criticize the government—essential freedoms that should not be compromised. Word quickly spread throughout student circles that the government had broken faith with the students and tricked them into dispersing. The student leaders of all the universities reconvened and planned another massive demonstration, announcing that this time they would not waste their time seeing the prime minister.

As the movement for the new protest gained momentum, the government suddenly held a high-level meeting and announced that the nine students would be readmitted without any conditions.[31] Ironically, at this crucial meeting none of the cabinet members even attempted to defend Dr. Sakdi, the rector. Moreover, some cabinet members encouraged the prime minister to remove Dr. Sakdi for the way he handled the entire matter. A few days later, Dr. Sakdi submitted his resignation. It was promptly accepted by the government.

In achieving all of the students' original demands without having to carry through with the planned follow-up demonstration, the unified and persistent nature of the movement was seen as a masterpiece of the National Student Center of Thailand. The government leaders were unable to sway the determination which marked this movement, even after the students had dispersed. The cooperation among the various universities in support of nine fellow students, as well as the swelling public support, gave an entirely new dimension to the strength and significance of the National Student Center of Thailand and its leadership in the politics of Thailand.

In the aftermath of this movement, however, there emerged another striking event. A group of students and professors protesting both the government's decision and the role of the National Student Center staged a counterdemonstration supporting Dr. Sakdi. Approximately a thousand Ramkamhaeng University students marched around the campus with placards and banners, one of which read: "We don't want those nine students!"[32] By midday the number of protesters had grown to about six thousand. After a rally held on campus the protesters decided to march to the prime minister's office, where they demanded to see Thanom. While waiting for a reply to their demand, they held a public forum and made speeches calling for the return of Dr. Sakdi and expulsion of the nine "troublemakers." Outside the prime minister's office the protesters periodically sang the King's Song and the national anthem to emphasize their loyalty to both king and country. The government was apparently unimpressed; it did not even send a representative to see them. The government did, however, let it be known that unless the protesters dispersed it would be forced to use violent measures to restore order. Several hours later, after much discussion and rumor, the counterdemonstration broke up and Dr. Sakdi's removal was upheld.

The organizational effort of the leaders of the National Student Center of Thailand had been praised by the government during Anti-Japanese Goods Week. Now, in the campaign to reinstate the Ramkamhaeng Nine, the National Student Center grudgingly won the government's respect as an effective oppositional force in the ever changing realm of Thai politics. Government leaders unofficially reported on the fearsome potential of organized student pressure in domestic politics. The NSCT was able, on occasion, to enlist considerable support from the working class, the middle class, and the intellectuals. Indeed, it was establishing itself as the voice of the people, promoting a democratic form of government in the face of a government determined to rule by martial law. This characterization of contemporary student activism in Thailand was explained in a special paper distributed by the National Student Center and written by its elected leader, Thirayuth Boonmee. In this paper, entitled "The Students Begin to Find Their Target," Thirayuth explains the relationship between the students and people:

> Nobody can hurt the students without hurting the people. This is because, first, students are the children of the people and, second, the people have

great faith in students. The students have proved that they are grateful for the taxes collected from the people for educational purposes. The students also try hard with all their ability to solve the many social problems. As long as the students stay on the people's side, the people's faith in them will remain. This will mean increased bargaining power with the government.[33]

About the students' perception of their own power, he writes:

Student activism can change society, as witnessed in Indonesia, Turkey, France, Japan, the United States, and other countries. We study and understand what has happened in other countries ... but I hope that the students do not overestimate their power. Power has to be controlled and used in a purposeful manner. Otherwise it can cause destruction and chaos. And this we do not want to see.[34]

On the future of the student movement, Thirayuth predicts with confidence:

We came through in the past and we shall not destroy our movement in the future.[35]

Thirayuth's confidence in the future of the student movement as a social and political force capable of changing the Thai political system soon became a reality. Less than five months after the major demonstration regarding the Ramkamhaeng Nine, Bangkok witnessed a violent student revolution which brought down the Thanom government and stopped military rule by martial law.[36]

Although this revolution was the outgrowth of yet another demonstration against the arbitrary decision of the military government and rule by martial law, its overriding significance to the Thai student movement and the future of the Thai political system merits special consideration here. The next section explains in detail the events leading up to the demonstration and subsequent violent revolution and depicts the political atmosphere in the immediate aftermath of the student revolt.

THE STUDENT REVOLT OF OCTOBER 1973

The fate of the Thanom military government and the future direction of the Thai political system were suddenly altered by a series of critical events which occurred between 6 and 15 October 1973. Commonly referred to as "The Ten Days," this period of 1973 may well become known as the most important series of events in Thai political history since the "revolution" of 1932. We turn now to an account of these eventful ten days.[37]

After the huge demonstration in June, Thirayuth Boonmee and other student leaders kept the pressure on the government to accelerate the promulgation of the constitution. On Saturday, 6 October 1973, Thirayuth and ten other political activists were arrested by special police agents while distributing leaflets urging support for the early drafting of the constitution. The leaflets specifically referred to 10 December 1973, Thailand's Constitution Day, as the date by which the constitution should be promulgated. Thirayuth and the other activists were accused of violating a National Executive Council decree which forbade more than five people to gather for political purposes. Those arrested with Thirayuth included Prapansak Kamolpetch, a former Bangkok parliamentary candidate, Boonsong Chalethorn, deputy secretary-general of the National Student Center, Bandhit Hengnilrat, a liberal arts student at Thammasat University, Visa Kanthap, a humanities student at Ramkamhaeng University, and Thanya Chunkathatharn, a writer for the weekly *Maharaj* magazine. Also arrested were Thawee Muenthikorn, a Thammasat economics instructor, Montri Juengsirinarak, a writer for the weekly *Social Science Review*, Nopporn Suwanpanich, a former Chulalongkorn arts instructor, Preedi Boonsue, a Thammasat political science student, and Chaiwat Suravichai, former vice-president of the Chulalongkorn Student Union.

Those arrested were first taken to police headquarters and thereafter escorted to their homes where detectives carried out an extensive search for "more incriminating evidence." In ordering the arrest of the students in lieu of freedom of assembly, and the search of their homes in lieu of freedom from unwarranted search and seizure, the Thanom–Prapas governing clique only added fuel to the flames of discontent and provided visible proof to the Thai public that student claims of government repression were correct. Moreover, when the military government ordered the confiscation of all leaflets calling for the promulgation of the permanent constitution as a matter of domestic security, it was quickly interpreted by the general Thai public as further evidence that Prime Minister Thanom Kittikachorn and Deputy Prime Minister Prapas Charusathien had no real intention of relinquishing their powerful positions to a constitutional government.

The train of government errors continued the following day, Sunday, 7 October 1973, when the deputy director general of the Police Department, Lt. Gen. Prachuab Suntharangkoon, ordered the arrest of Kongkiat Kongka, who was accused of being an outspoken member of another activist group demanding early promulgation of the permanent constitution. Meanwhile, on this same day, the leaders of the powerful National Student Center of Thailand threatened retaliation for the government's actions.

Setting the Stage for Confrontation

The stage was being set for confrontation as the government continued to remain insensitive to students' demands and apparently ignorant of their determination. This was clearly seen the next day, Monday, 8 October 1973, when Prapas ruled out the possibility of early bail for the twelve arrested activists and publicly announced that confiscated documents linked the twelve with a plot to overthrow the government. Prapas, in a further attempt to retrieve public support for the government's seemingly repressive acts, claimed that the police had seized documents "about communism" in both Thai and Chinese. The Student Organization of the National Institute of Development Administration also appealed to Prime Minister Thanom to drop the charge of inciting the public to act, but the government refused.

The implication by Prapas that the activists were engaged in some communist-inspired plot only angered the students further, and on the following day, Tuesday, 9 October 1973, more than two thousand Thammasat University students congregated for an antigovernment rally. Meanwhile, the entire metropolitan police force was put on full alert as police received reports that the students threatened to march to Bang Khen detention center where the twelve arrested activists were being held. Thammasat students also symbolically registered their disgust with the government by lowering the national flag and putting up a black flag as a sign of mourning. Although the black flag was removed by Thammasat University authorities, students refused to attend classes to take their first-semester examinations, which had to be called off for an indefinite period. In the meantime, small groups of students went to Bang Khen to visit the arrested activists but were allowed to see only five of the twelve. The continued refusal of the police to allow personal visits to the remaining seven activists (among them Thirayuth) eventually led to rumors late in the week that they had been seriously tortured or even killed in captivity.

During the afternoon of 9 October, the Thammasat Student Legislative Body voted approval of a four-point proposal to be carried out by the Thammasat Student Council. These points were:

1. Nonviolent protests will be made first, and the students will remain at the Photi compound until the release of the twelve detainees.
2. Ten representatives will be appointed to negotiate with the government for a speedy release of the twelve detainees.
3. Letters will be sent to all universities and institutes, calling for a show of strength and unity to support the negotiations.
4. If the government still refuses to release the twelve after these nonvio-

lent protests have been made, the students will resort to violence in the form of demonstrations and bloodshed.

Rallies were held on other campuses on 9 October, but the topics of protest were not always political. The case of one very practical group of students at Prasammitra Teachers College was reported by the *Bangkok Post* as follows:

> Several student leaders voiced their opinion during a mass student rally at the college yesterday that toilets are most important during student demonstrations. They pointed out that past demonstrations showed the marchers could not hold on longer than a few days since all of them have to go to toilets, change their clothes, and brush their teeth. They reasoned that if movable toilets are set up at the demonstration sites, the marchers could hold on longer in their fight for justice and democracy....[38]

After the rallies, students from Thammasat and Chulalongkorn universities and several of the teacher training colleges of Bangkok joined in an all-night vigil, braving the cold and light showers, and vowed "full support" to those arrested. The arrested now included a former member of Parliament, Khaisaeng Suksai, as the list of political prisoners climbed to thirteen.

The following morning, 10 October 1973, the students made good their promise of support and an additional thousand students joined in the protest rallies. Much to the satisfaction of the swelling crowds, student leaders declared that the Thanom–Prapas clique had staged the revolution "of itself, for itself, and by itself." As the crowds at the rallies continued to grow throughout the afternoon, with mounting tension, the government announced that Deputy Prime Minister Prapas had been appointed head of a special independent organization to "restore peace and order." At the same time, the commander-in-chief of the Royal Thai Army, General Kris Sivara, was named as Marshal Prapas's deputy in the new suppression force which had its headquarters, interestingly enough, at the Communist Suppression Operations Command (CSOC).

On the following day, 11 October 1973, Prapas agreed to meet with student representatives of the National Student Center of Thailand, who promptly demanded the release of the thirteen political prisoners. Prapas refused the demand but vowed to have a constitution ready in twenty months. When asked why Article 17, which allowed arrest and detention without due process, was invoked against the political activists, Prapas explained that it was for the benefit of the detainees because authorities would be empowered to expedite the case without going through normal legal procedure in postponing litigation. Thai student leaders remained unimpressed with the government's attempt at negotiation and were particularly perturbed with Prapas's refusal to release the thirteen political activists. They returned to the rally, which had now moved to the Thammasat University football grounds to accommodate the growing crowd of more than fifty thousand, to announce that the NSCT would take sole responsibility for the school closures and student walkouts. At that point about 70 percent of all private and government schools in Bangkok had already called off classes either by official order or by action taken by the students to join forces with the NSCT at the Thammasat campus.

In the meantime, the thirteen political activists being held at the Metropolitan Police Training School in Bang Khen staged a hunger strike to protest the delay in police investigations and to give moral support to the mass rally of students. Seemingly worried over the course of events, Prime Minister Thanom and Deputy Prime Minister Prapas consulted with the king in a special audience that evening at Chitrlada Palace. In a discussion which lasted about two hours, the king reportedly expressed grave concern over the present student uprising.

The next morning, in a move which was apparently designed to avoid confrontation with the students, the government made an announcement: "If any investigations show that the students were purely and sincerely demanding the constitution, they will be released with fines for holding a political gathering of more than five persons." Making a clear distinction between young students and adult politicians, however, the government maintained that legal action would be taken against the eight politicians who were arrested if they were found guilty as charged.

It was apparently an offer of too little and too late, for the day began in a frenzy as thousands of students from universities, technical colleges, teachers training colleges, vocational colleges, and secondary schools streamed toward the Thammasat University rendezvous from all directions. Many of the students arrived on foot, often accompanied by sympathetic teachers and lecturers while several passersby donated money to the marchers. The number of students pouring into the Thammasat grounds swelled to tens of thousands by midday as it was announced that all schools in Bangkok had been closed indefinitely. Chulalongkorn University and Ramkamhaeng University also announced the indefinite postponement of all examinations. Moreover, the Chulalongkorn Student Union declared in a formal statement that they "openly opposed" the government's action on the arrests, as "they could not bear the injustice any longer."

Meanwhile, the students stepped up the pressure on the government by announcing a demand for the unconditional release of the thirteen detainees. The NSCT gave a 24-hour deadline starting from midday and warned of "decisive action" if the demand was not met. The director-general of the Public Relations Department, Maj. Gen. Prakob Charumanee, issued an assurance that no force would be used against the demonstrating students, and he appealed to the public to avoid the congested area around Thammasat University. An extraordinary emergency cabinet meeting was called at the Communist Suppression Operations Command at 2:00 P.M. to consider the ultimatum. The meeting went on for several hours before a solution was found; meanwhile, at Thammasat, tension was building as students waited for an answer from the government on their demands. An hour-by-hour countdown was started as student leaders informed the crowd that there were 23 ... 22 ... 21 ... hours to the deadline.

On the evening of 12 October 1973, about five hours after the ultimatum was received by the government, it was announced to the waiting students that the thirteen political activists would be released on bail. A great cheer went up around the crowded field as most students appeared satisfied. Some student leaders were still disgruntled, however, pointing out to the rally that they had demanded an unconditional release, not release on bail. One of the thirteen activists being held by the government, Chaiwat Suravichai, was sent to explain the situation. At the rally he indicated that the other twelve prisoners were willing to remain in the detention center and that their release should not affect the continued protests for an early promulgation of the constitution. After hours of debate, the majority of the students present decided to reject the bail offer. At 11:25 P.M. the remaining twelve political activists, upon learning of the NSCT's decision, refused to sign a paper accepting their temporary release.

This offer, though not all that the students wanted, was obviously as far as the government was prepared to go. Using previous demonstrations as a yardstick for compromise, the government obviously felt that release of the thirteen activists would allow both the students and government to save face while avoiding a violent confrontation. This time, however, the government gravely underestimated the determination of the students on the constitutional issue. Discontent among students and the Thai public at large had reached an all-time high, and student leaders were well aware of the implications and power of their position. Moreover, they had been misled by promises of release just three months before in the case of the Ramkamhaeng Nine. They were not about to disperse as they had in the last demonstration and relinquish their powerful position, only to have the government renege on its promises. After the students flatly refused to accept anything less than unconditional release of the thirteen, the government found itself with an uncomfortable choice: either complete loss of face or an impressive show of force. In choosing the latter, they set the final stage for confrontation.

Confrontation and Violence

At 11:30 on the morning of 13 October 1973, soldiers took up positions along the perimeter of the Communist Suppression Operations Command headquarters while the twelve remaining activists stayed on the grass outside the Bang Khen detention center refusing to go with the police to Patumwan headquarters. They were waiting for activist Chaiwat to return with the results of his discussion with protesting students at Thammasat University. About a half hour later, the government announced that it would not back down on its refusal to release the thirteen activists unconditionally. About the same time, all gates leading to Thammasat University were closed as the demonstrators took up their positions. As a result, Chaiwat was unable to leave Thammasat to rejoin the other twelve activists, who at this point had gone back into their detention cell and refused to leave.

While the students were completing their plans to make the customary march along Rajdamnern Avenue, pandemonium nearly broke out at Bang Khen as police, under the direction of the Special Branch police commander, Maj. Gen. Chai Suwansnasorn, tried to persuade the twelve activists to leave since they were officially released on bail. A team of more than twenty commandos entered the cell where the twelve activists were staying. After heated discussions, the twelve activists, including Thirayuth Boonmee, voluntarily walked out from the detention center and waited patiently near the superhighway for a "final decision" from the National Student Center of Thailand. When word came, however, that the student demonstration had gained momentum, most of the detainees joined the NSCT leaders near Thammasat.

In the meantime, some 200,000 protesting students left Thammasat University campus in a protest march to demand the unconditional release of the thirteen activists. Preparations were made for a prolonged demonstration at Thammasat University as the NSCT food and welfare committees loaded about ten small pickup trucks with food, fruit, and other necessary supplies. The chairman of the Constitutional Drafting Committee of the NSCT, Rachan Wiraphan, said that if the thirteen constitutional activists were not released by noon the students would march to the Parliament Building. He also revealed an alternative plan which called for the marchers to rally at the Democracy Monument if they were blocked by government forces on Rajdamnern Avenue at

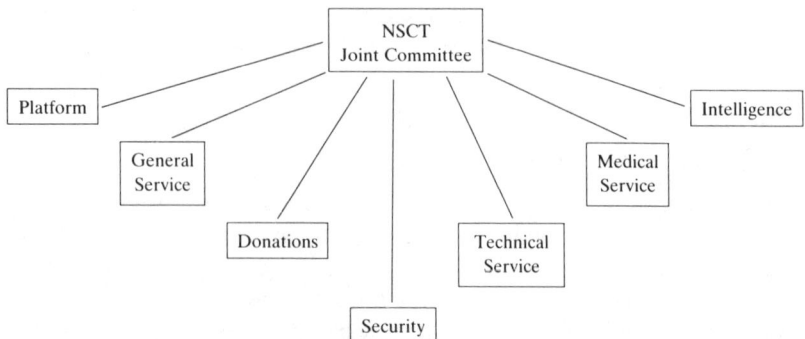

Figure 3   Organization of the NSCT during the five-day protest

Makkhawan Bridge. The strategy for the organized protest directed each university and school participating in the demonstration to assemble in a specific area so that leaders could detect any "third hands." Tough engineering students were to make up the front column of the protest march in case of clashes with government forces.

As the march began, it became obvious that the NSCT leaders had been meticulous in their plans. First a group of scouts was sent ahead to clear the way for the protest march. Groups of students were organized into separate sections to be responsible for food, first aid, coordination, commando duties, and so forth, each with its own colored armbands. (See Figure 3.) Some engineering students carried wooden or metal bars while others wore protection against tear gas. A group of girl students marched ahead of the column carrying pictures of the king and queen. Close behind the girls was a group of young men with thick sacks for placing on barbed wire obstacles and for throwing over police dogs. This group was referred to as the "antidog" unit. Small groups of first aid workers walked among the marchers holding Red Cross flags aloft for easy identification. While the students were protesting peacefully at Sanam Luang and Rajdamnern Avenue, the king met with an NSCT delegation of nine, among them some of the released activists from Bang Khen center.

Meanwhile, public support swelled as large amounts of cash, food, and supplies flowed into the donation booths in and around Thammasat University. By noon the NSCT announced it had collected more than 400,000 baht (approximately $20,000). It was also reported that the majority of Bangkok buslines running to the Sanam Luang area would not pick up passengers other than those going to Thammasat University, and bus conductors were turning away passengers who indicated they were not going to attend the rally. The conductor of a packed bus which avoided the regular bus stops and went directly to Thammasat University simply explained his behavior by asserting that "we are all fighting for the constitution."

Before the protesting marchers, now more than 400,000 strong, moved from the Democracy Monument, there was news that the government had agreed to the NSCT demand calling for the unconditional release of the thirteen activists. The students had gained an important victory involving the unconditional release of the activists. Although the activists had already been released on bail and allowed to leave the detention center, they would eventually have had to face the charges in court. The government also promised that the permanent constitution would be promulgated by October 1974. Having achieved what they considered a victory, the student leaders called off the demonstration at the Democracy Monument and returned to Thammasat University to celebrate.

More than 200,000 students remained on the streets, however, and thousands of them refused to disband. This group, which included the hard-core vocational and engineering students, was under the direction of Seksan Prasertjul, a student of political science at Thammasat University.[39] These students were dissatisfied and wanted a guarantee that the government would keep its promises to the students. Seksan tried to control the restless crowd, urging them to avoid any violent measure and attempting meanwhile to reach the other leaders of the NSCT, but his efforts were in vain. At about twelve o'clock, midnight, Seksan decided to lead the crowd to the royal palace to request the king's advice. At that point some of the other leaders of the NSCT showed up and tried to persuade the crowd to go home and not follow Seksan. After Seksan and other leaders of the NSCT, including the former secretary-general, met and discussed what had happened, however, the two sides reached an understanding. What actually went on at this meeting is still open to question, but according to some of the student leaders two major points were discussed.

In the first place, since their personal safety was not guaranteed by the government there seemed to be little advantage to disbanding. Second, it was generally agreed that if confrontation was going to occur it should take place near the palace so that retreating students could take refuge in the palace grounds. This strategy, though a departure from all previous routes of confrontation which usually bypassed the palace in favor of the government buildings, was actually part of a contingency plan. The leaders in their meeting discussed this plan along with other proposals, many of which reflected the writings of a famous Thai revolutionist known only as "Jit" to many of the student leaders. This brilliant student of Chulalongkorn University, upon graduation, chose communist insurrection in the jungle rather than the Thai bureaucracy in Bangkok. After his death in 1967 in a fight with government forces, his writings, representing a blueprint for the Thai peoples' revolution, began to emerge in books and newspapers around the university campuses. It is noteworthy that the events which followed this meeting are neatly outlined in several of these revolutionary essays.

It was still the same fateful Sunday morning of 14 October when the students reached the palace. Only the king's representative, however, Col. Vasit Dejkunchorn, came to see them about 5:30 A.M. This representative read the king's advice to the students—which was to disband peacefully since the thirteen activists had been unconditionally released and the constitution had been promised before October. After reading this message, Colonel Vasit told the students that "their majesties had been unable to sleep for four nights running during the protest. Now the king would like all of you to go home."

It looked for a moment as though the situation would return to normal as the students themselves, after singing the national anthem together, prepared to go home. As the demonstrators started to disband, however, an unfortunate incident triggered a violent riot which was to last for the next two days. When the demonstrators attempted to leave the street in front of the palace, Lt. Gen. Monchai Phankongchuen, assistant director of the police department, ordered his men to form a barricade so that the students should leave the area in only one direction to ensure an orderly dispersal. The mass of students, however, proved too large, and when the students' request that another exit should be allowed was refused, a wave of resentment ran through the mass of demonstrators.

It was about 6:30 A.M. when this confrontation turned into a violent clash. Exactly what happened has been reported in various ways. Some eyewitnesses claim that the police began clubbing the demonstrators because they were shoving against the police line. A reporter at the scene claimed that a bag of ice thrown from the crowd hit a policeman squarely on the head and knocked him down, after which the police began using tear gas and threatened the students with their weapons. In any event, Molotov cocktails started flying in the direction of the police, while the police opened fire on the students. Many demonstrators were injured as some attempted to fight back with wooden clubs. Most of the students, however, attempted to run from the area. Some jumped into the moat nearby while others ran to take refuge inside the palace grounds.[40] Three girl students were said to have been beaten to death by the police.[41] Many of the demonstrators ran back to the Parliament Building while some returned to the Democracy Monument and others to Thammasat University. They quickly spread the news of police brutality in the palace clash. The story about the girls being beaten to death was told and retold.

The demonstrators were now without leaders as all NSCT officials had disappeared from the crowd. Seksan was said to have collapsed from exhaustion due to his intense and continued activity in the last four to five days.

Meanwhile, at Thammasat campus, the students started to regroup, anxious to gain revenge on the police for their brutality. At about 7:45 A.M., a group of demonstrators set fire to a police booth beside Thammasat University. From that time on the violent clashes between students, who were joined by the public, and government forces continued along Rajdamnern Avenue for two days and one night. The heaviest fighting occurred near the end of Rajdamnern Avenue in the proximity of Pramain Ground. The government brought several tanks and some five hundred soldiers to the aid of the Bangkok police force in combating the demonstrators. The demonstrators refused to disband, however, and many fought back with wooden clubs while a few had pistols. When the demonstrators were first confronted by the tanks, they thought the soldiers would not actually use them against students. This assumption proved false, however, as the army fired M-16 rifles and tank machine guns into the crowds of demonstrators. These weapons, along with the government's helicopter gunships, were responsible for most of the casualties.[42] Several hundred students were shot and wounded; more than one hundred were killed. A small number of soldiers was also killed or injured.

Throughout the violent confrontation, the government used the media to broadcast news reports claiming that the demonstrators were not students but communist agents and that the student leaders had been forced to join a plot to overthrow the government. The government greatly exaggerated the rioters' capabilities by claiming that some demonstrators possessed machine guns and had killed many soldiers. The broadcasts never gave any account of the number of demonstrators killed or wounded.

At about 3:30 P.M. the military gained control of Thammasat University, and large numbers of demonstrators had to withdraw across the Chao Phraya River, jamming the Pran Nok landing. As the demonstrators realized the futility of fighting tanks and machine guns with clubs and Molotov cocktails, they turned their frustration on other symbols of government authority. Many of the government buildings along Rajdamnern Avenue were set afire as people from all over Bangkok traveled to the scene of the fighting. The mass of demonstrators and onlookers grew to over half a million people as crowds began to pour into Rajdamnern Avenue. Finally, at about 5:30 P.M. on 14 October, the government gave up the battle and the soldiers were ordered to withdraw from Rajdamnern Avenue.

At about the same time, the government announced over Radio Thailand that it had tendered its resignation to the king. At about 7:15 P.M. the king addressed the nation on television and all radio stations, officially announcing that Thanom's government had resigned and Professor Sanya Thammasakdi, the rector of Thammasat University, had been appointed as the new prime minister. At that point, many people cheered and ran into the streets shouting victory. Late that night Professor Sanya addressed the nation by television and radio, promising a constitution and election within six months.

Thereafter thousands of students and other demonstrators congregated at Democracy Monument where speakers were asking them to disband and go home. Many students, however, were still angry over the slaughter of hundreds of young and unarmed people. They argued that it was not enough that the government had resigned as long as Field Marshal Thanom remained supreme commander of the armed forces and Prapas was still director general of the Police Department. Many demonstrators wanted to continue the protest until they were sure that Thanom and Prapas were powerless; others wanted to see both men dead. The hard-core "Yellow Tiger" commando unit of the students directed their hostility to the metropolitan police headquarters, which was now symbolic of the entire police force. The police protecting the headquarters had machine guns; several students had rifles and pistols.[43]

The gun battle between students and police in and around the police headquarters lasted from late on 14 October until the following afternoon. At 7:00 A.M. on 15 October, the commando students at Phanfa Bridge were still holding out but were planning to retreat to the Democracy Monument. It was reported that a doctor, a medical assistant, and five nurses had been shot dead near the bridge by what was believed to be machine gun and M-16 rifle fire as they were tending to casualties in the "battlefield" facing the metropolitan police headquarters several hours before dawn. As the battle ensued, hundreds of demonstrators were gunned down as they tried to close in on the police headquarters.

Finally the police abandoned the building when the students set it afire. The technique they employed was as ingenious as it was daring. After hijacking a fire engine at the scene, the Yellow Tiger squad emptied the water from the tanks and siphoned gasoline from a nearby gas station. They then sent a jet of the high-octane gasoline from a fire engine hose into the metropolitan police headquarters near the bridge and tossed Molotov cocktails into the pool of gasoline. An eyewitness at the scene said, "Some were shot down, but the remainder successfully sent gasoline from a powerful hose into the building and then set in on fire."[44] In the meantime, rioting students and the public, many of them in their teens, roamed the streets, packed into commandeered buses and trucks, and burned down or smashed most of the city's police booths, traffic lights, and traffic signs.

At about 9:00 P.M., an unexpected calm came over the rioters when it was announced via radio and television that Field Marshal Thanom Kittikachorn, Field Marshal Prapas Charusathien and Colonel Narong Kittikachorn had left the country.[45] As the gatherings dissolved, bus companies joined army buses in giving students free rides home while other students remained to direct traffic and put out the fires. It was clearly a victory for the students and other demonstrating civilians. Not a single uniformed policeman was in sight on the streets of Bangkok. One student, armed with a fire hose to fight the flames which still raged along Rajdamnern Avenue, summed up the significance of these historic ten days in October when he remarked, "We have made a new Thailand but it cost us a lot."[46]

The Revolt in Retrospect

While the role of the students in overthrowing the military government was no doubt the most significant contribution to its downfall, there were other groups and certain conditions which aided the students' cause. A major supporting condition was the growing cleavages within the military itself which had undermined much of the support for the Thanom and Prapas regime. The Royal Thai Navy, which had remained subservient to the powerful army cliques ever since the "*Manhattan Affair*,"[47] openly supported the students' cause. Even within the army and the air force there were officers who found reasons not to come to the aid of the police force while it was under siege by the students. The intellectuals and former opposition politicians also helped the students' cause. Common laborers and other civilian workers who went out on wildcat strikes in August and September aided in creating the atmosphere for revolt, and many of these people also participated in the demonstrations against the government in October.

The overall effect of the efforts of the students and their supporters was the creation of a free but chaotic atmosphere in the immediate aftermath of the revolt, at which time the NSCT and other breakaway student groups attempted to consolidate their power. More important, the student revolution created in its aftermath at least the atmosphere, for change. Significant steps toward the establishment of democratic institutions could now be taken.

Student Activism after the October Revolt

The successful student revolt of October 1973 marked a significant departure from all previous changes of government in Thailand. The new government was not only run by civilians but it had ascended to dominance through the efforts of a prolonged and well-organized demonstration led by students. Moreover, the victory for the civilian-led government was obtained at the expense of the army and the police even though these two groups were in complete control of a government ruling by martial law. This was no small accomplishment, and the students were quick to grasp the implications of their increased power base. While the period immediately following the formation of a civilian government showed a sudden decrease in general civilian protests and related political activities, there was a steady increase in student activism and protest demonstrations throughout the country.

In the months immediately following Sanya Thammasakdi's accession to the post of prime minister, student protests were mounted against provincial governors, high-ranking university officials and other educators, a major Thai newspaper, the United States ambassador, and certain American military officials. One such protest occurred on 21 October and involved an estimated five thousand students in the northern province of Lamphun. Students demanded and obtained the resignation of the governor, Rond Thasanachalee, for alleged corruption in administering a fund allocated for local school projects.

More important than the shift in government officials at the top of the bureaucracy was the fact that the appointment process, so prevalent in the Thai bureaucracy, was overruled in favor of a democratic elective process. As this system of selection became accepted, it permeated various levels of the government bureaucracy in other educational and service-oriented institutions. Moreover, significant changes began to take place in making the traditional bureaucracy more accountable. While there were early indications that other institutions (such as Kasetsart University) were ready to adopt the new system, there were also signs of resistance to this system by those who maintained that it was incompatible with Thai culture. In the meantime, student leaders blacklisted many of the high-ranking officials in the bureaucracy. Although the students were seldom able to have these people removed from government service, they did manage to have many of them transferred to less sensitive positions in some of the most remote provinces of Thailand. The students therefore effectively utilized the age-old bureaucratic technique of transfer in order to remove many supporters of the Thanom–Prapas clique.

Some student leaders, however, realized the necessity to change the *cultural* values of the established authorities, particularly those of the educational administrators. An informal practice which eventually came to be known as *lang kru* ("washing" or "cleanup") began to be carried out by students at every level of the Thai education system, particularly in the universities and high schools. The ostensible purpose of the "washing" exercise was to modernize teacher attitudes toward students and to promote student-oriented programs. Moreover, it grew out of the students' desire to have teachers understand their values, behavior, and aspirations. The harsher interpretation of *lang kru*, however, is to "clean out," by removal or transfer, teachers seen as corrupt or reactionary. Protest leaders realized that if permanent acceptance, tacit or real, of the democratic innovations proposed by the students was to become a reality, change in various crucial levels of the Thai bureaucracy had to take place.

Another significant departure from all previous Thai student movements was the emergence of influential independent student organizations which broke away from the moderate centrist positions of the National Student Center of Thailand. The most significant of these organizations was the Free Thammasat Movement led by Seksan, the political science student who played a significant role in the demonstrations leading to the overthrow of the military regime. A close affiliate of the Free Thammasat Movement and an apparent counterpart at Chulalongkorn University was the Independent Chulalongkorn Student Group. Both student organizations were extremely nationalistic, and both supported more socialistic positions on domestic issues and anti-imperialistic positions on foreign policy issues than did the National Student Center.

A New Wave of Protest

These two groups continue to be in the vanguard of the protest demonstrations for structural and policy changes in Thai government. In fact, it was the Independent Chulalongkorn Student Group which launched a citywide protest against the newly appointed American ambassador William Kinter in mid-November 1973. Posters demanding "Chase Kinter Away!" were displayed around the Chulalongkorn University campus while students distributed more than thirty thousand leaflets at all the thoroughfares in Bangkok. The leaflets described Kinter as a career military man and warned the Thai people that the new U.S. ambassador would be "war-minded" in his approach. Kinter had been a colonel in the U.S. Army, in fact, and had also worked for the CIA for two years in Washington. The leaflets further attacked American "imperialism" and contended that:

> American intervention in Indochina has caused adverse effects on Thailand. Support for the previous military government has led to the decay of democracy in Thailand, and American bases here have tarnished the good image of Thailand as an independent country.[48]

It took less than two months for Ambassador Kinter to fulfill the students' prophecy of intervention, for a widely publicized CIA blunder provided adequate proof that this agency was in fact meddling in the affairs of the Thai government. The bizarre incident involved a CIA agent whose base of operation was the provincial town of Sakhon Nakhon in northeastern Thailand, an area where communist insurgents had steadily increased their activities. The agent apparently sent a phony letter to Prime Minister Sanya Thammasakdi, and several newspapers as well, proposing a cease-fire with the insurgents in exchange for granting autonomy to rebels in Thailand's northeastern provinces. The letter from the CIA agent was sent in the name of the local rebel commander of the estimated five thousand communist insurgents in Sakhon Nakhon.

The CIA's involvement was revealed by an apparent blunder by a messenger boy who had the letter registered—thereby allowing Thai officials to trace it to the CIA office in Sakhon Nakhon. While Ambassador Kinter, in his official apology to the Thai government, described the agent's actions as a "regrettable" and "unauthorized initiative," suspicious Thai officials wisely surmised that the letter was designed to assess the new government's response to a cease-fire with the communists. Apparently the students also realized that the most regrettable aspect of the incident, as far as the U.S. embassy was concerned, was the fact that the CIA agent's activities had been exposed. With the support of most of the Thai-language newspapers, the students launched a series of protest activities directed at U.S. intervention in Thai affairs. On 6 January 1974, Thai students laid a wreath in front of the embassy bearing the slogan "Go home, ugly Americans." The newspapers, meanwhile, carried anti-CIA editorials and cartoons.[49]

Hoping to stem the tide of anti-CIA and anti-American sentiment which was on the rise after the incident, Ambassador Kinter disclosed on 8 January that the CIA agent responsible for the letter had been transferred out of Thailand, and an embassy spokesman revealed that "appropriate disciplinary action" was being taken. The students were apparently unimpressed with Kinter's explanation, however, for on the very next night, 9 January, some five thousand students protested at the U.S. embassy grounds while student leaders attacked the CIA over a public address system outside the embassy gates. More important, several days after the CIA incident senior Thai officials revealed that the CIA would be told to close its field posts and stay out of Thailand's internal affairs.

Previously the CIA had enjoyed the Thai government's cooperation for most of its clandestine activities. Operating out of the political section on the fourth floor of the U.S. embassy under the agency's Plans Directorate, the department became known as the "dirty tricks department." The CIA operation in Thailand had been one of the agency's largest overseas units and had cultivated an exceptionally close relationship with the former Thai prime minister, Thanom Kittikachorn. According to informed Thai sources, the relationship was so close that Thanom often made himself more available to the CIA chief than to the U.S. ambassador.

During the same tumultuous weeks of the CIA incident, thousands of Thai students gave Japanese Prime Minister Tanaka a hostile reception as he arrived in Bangkok for a two-day visit. The students massed outside Tanaka's hotel, blocked all the entrances with buses, and demanded that Tanaka leave the country immediately. They withdrew that threat and moved the buses only after Japan's ambassador accepted a list of demands from them. These demands included:

1. All Japanese loans to Thailand must be without conditions.
2. Japan must lift its import quotas on Thai products.
3. The Japanese government must educate all prospective Japanese investors in Thailand regarding Thailand's needs, traditions, and culture.

Thereafter the students allowed Tanaka to leave his hotel, but as he left they beat on his limousine and shouted "Japanese go home!" The police did not interfere; only student marshals with red armbands held back the noisy crowd of students who began burning paper effigies of Japanese cars in front of the nearby Japanese Trade Center.

During the months following the student revolt, a major student protest was also launched against Thailand's most influential Thai-language newspaper, *Siam Rath*, because of a letter critical of King Bhumibhol. Two Thais in Sweden had criticized the king for not controlling troops and police during the student revolt in October 1973. At a student rally, the newspaper was publicly burned as a symbol of the students' discontent with the letter and determination to censor the editor from further publication. Shortly thereafter, the Thai police suspended the editor's license indefinitely for having published the letter. The editor, Nopporn Boonyarit, tried in vain to defend himself by asserting that the paper was simply trying to expose attempts to undermine the monarchy.

The monarchy, and particularly the present king, has always commanded significant respect and admiration from all Thai student movements. King Bhumibhol has been continually involved in public activities, especially those related to Thailand's youth. Moreover, since his accession in 1955 he has personally presented the diploma to every university graduate in the country. A photograph snapped of each presentation is hung on the walls of around fifteen thousand Thai homes every year. While the student protest was an attack on the newspaper *Siam Rath* and in support of the king, it had the intended effect of putting all newspapers on notice that public criticism of those people and ideals held sacred by the new student revolution would not be tolerated. Growing intolerance of criticism directed at student-supported individuals and ideals became more significant as the student leaders continued in their strategy to change the Thai society and political system.

The Role of the NSCT

Public support for the main student organization, the NSCT, continued after the October uprising. In fact, by December 1973 the NSCT had received almost 20 million baht (approximately $1 million in U.S. currency) in donations from the public. Some of the money was used to help the families of those who were killed during the uprising; other funds went toward paying the medical bills of demonstrators who were injured. The NSCT also set aside a huge sum as a proposed budget for the Teaching Democracy Program which was to take place during the 1973–1974 academic year, and university authorities cooperated with the proposed program by rescheduling classes for students who wished to participate.

The NSCT's Teaching Democracy Program was originally designed to have people in all the provinces become aware of the purpose and political implications of democratic insitutions and principles. The students had planned to bring the message to the people through the use of several thousand dedicated NSCT members who could spend their time and energy "teaching democracy" in the outer provinces and remote villages of Thailand. The "teaching democracy" aspects of the program became somewhat misleading, however, and after initial setbacks the student leaders and advisors who were promoting the program adjusted their objectives to provincial conditions. Before the program had officially begun, FIST, the newly formed breakaway student group from the NSCT, under Seksan's leadership decided to carry their cause to the provinces. The westernized middle-class and urban background which characterized many students of this group hindered them from establishing the necessary rapport with the common people of the provinces, however.

Learning primarily from the mistakes and successes of Seksan's experiment and the performance (or lack of it in many cases) of the Democracy Development Program of the late 1960s, the Teaching Democracy Program was redirected in the form of a domestic Peace Corps with a predominant philosophy approaching thought reform. To establish rapport with villagers, some five thousand students were selected for specific assignments on the basis of their knowledge of the province in question. Hence an attempt was made to assign students from the northeast and south and other provincial areas to their home towns; rather than "teach democracy," they were to reacquaint themselves with the concerns of the villagers. Moreover, students from metropolitan Bangkok were urged to shed their urban and Western life-styles and live like the people whose interests they wish to serve and to listen to the villagers' problems before discussing politics. Student leaders believed that the success of their cultural revolution in the provinces would, in large part, determine the permanency of the political changes they had already achieved as well as the acceptance of effective constitutional government in the future.

The Reemergence of Parliament

Serious problems soon arose, however, since the military leaders were not ready to acquiesce mildly to the results of the new order of government for any length of time. The military had played a significant role in the Thai government's decision-making process since 1932, and it was reasonable to assume that they would remain a major influence in the shaping of the new government in the future. In 1974 there was considerable speculation that the military would resort to a coup if the demonstrations became more violent or were directed against the present military leaders or in the event that the ongoing student movement became exceedingly leftist in nature and tactics.

As the proposed campaigns and platforms of the Prachatipat and various other political parties began to enfold and dominate the media in February and March of 1974, the role of student leaders and activists became increasingly vague. The Thai public and media, which had steadfastly supported the students on almost every issue before, during, and after the October revolution of 1973, began to turn their attention to the upcoming elections and criticize the behavior and proposals of student leaders.

Moreover, it seemed as though the public had begun to show weariness with the many strikes, demonstrations, and the sometimes violent fighting among students from various vocational schools which had become commonplace in the three months which followed the October revolt. Since the military had been overthrown and the new constitution was already drafted, the public seemed to feel that the students had accomplished their main mission. Therefore, in view of rising inflation, the energy crisis, and a sagging economy, the Thai public became more interested in practical solutions and traditional approaches to political change.

The student leaders, however, remained determined to continue the movement even though it had lost much of its momentum by March 1974. Students began to attack various activities of the government and business leaders in search of an issue that would gain nationwide support. With the major opposition—the former military ruling clique—no longer in power, even the moderate NSCT had a difficult time persuading a public suffering from a major economic depression to support them on various idealistic issues.

Events in Thailand in the months of May and June 1974 increased the power of the moderately liberal civilian government. A brief military alert after the resignation of Sanya and his cabinet gave rise to speculation about a return to military rule, but Sanya was persuaded to resume office and, in doing so, rid the cabinet of all remnants of the old military regime. In their place he appointed younger and moderately liberal persons of high integrity. In the meantime, organized student groups began to ally themselves with worker and farmer causes. They were successful in organizing strikes among textile and other workers and forced the resignation of several high-ranking government officials.

The Sanya government and the Thai bureaucracy continued to avoid confrontation by appeasing the new forces on the left. Between October 1973 and June 1975, about 90 percent of the demands of all major protest movements by students, workers, and farmers were eventually met by the government. Overall this period of transition witnessed an unprecedented proliferation of interest groups in Thai politics. The prospects of some of the new groups, moreover, began to improve at the expense of old established groups. While for the most part violent confrontation between these old and new forces was avoided during this period, the prospects for a stable government and a lasting parliamentary democracy became a major concern of the 1975 elections.

The election of 1975 was to be an important step in the process of building lasting democratic institutions, and many university students and intellectuals helped organize and support the new socialist-oriented political parties (the Socialist Party of Thailand, New Force Party, Farmers Party, and others). The campaign and elections of 1975 also created an atmosphere for participation of previously unrepresented sectors of Thai society.

Between 1973 and 1976, student activism as well as all other forms of protest behavior against the government gained momentum and became a significant means for political change in Thailand. Workers, farmers, fishermen, teachers, and numerous other grass-roots organizations began to mobilize and press demands upon the fragile civilian governments of Sanya Thammasakdi (1973–1975), Seni Pramoj (1975), and Kukrit Pramoj (1975–1976).[50] By 1975, student protests had become more radical and leftist in orientation and tactics. Leadership of the student body at Thammasat University in 1975, for example, claimed to be Maoist and promoted anti-imperialist, antimilitary, and anticapitalist demonstrations. Some student factions even claimed to be antimonarchy.[51] In attempting to promote their socialist causes, some of these politically conscious students from Thammasat were resisted by right-wing student groups and often confrontation and violence resulted. This was the case in October 1976 when a mass protest demonstration by students at Thammasat University led to a bloody battle between leftist students, right-wing youth groups, and the police. The battle at Thammasat precipitated a declaration of martial law by military leaders, the end to the newly elected government of Seni Pramoj, the closing of Parliament, and an end to all other forms of political participation by students, workers, and farmers.

Return to the Right: 1976–1979

After the 1976 clash between students and the police, the staunchly conservative regime of Thanin Kraivixien began a campaign to suppress all forms of activism by students, workers, and farmers. It was during this period (1976–1979) that numerous assassinations took place, particularly among leaders of various farmers' organizations. It was also during this period that many of the student leaders and a few labor leaders and socialist politicians fled to the jungle and joined the Communist Party of Thailand. Most notable among the students who decided to continue their struggle in the jungle with the communists were Thirayuth and Seksan, who eventually became prominent members of CPT front organizations in 1977.

Meanwhile, student-initiated activism at the major universities involving political issues was reduced to nil. Political campaigns and elections, which have traditionally been a means of student leaders to revitalize student interest and activism, failed to attract participation in 1979.

In fact, in the 1979 campaigns and elections university students were most conspicuous by their absence.⁵²

The years from 1976 to 1979 seemed like a return to the late 1960s as student activities on the Thai university campuses were manifested in nonpolitical issues such as degree requirements. Moreover, most violent confrontations occurred among students from different universities or among students from various disciplines at the same university. Unrest among Thai university students in 1978–1980 was characterized by battles involving vocational and engineering students over traditional university rivalries and included the use of guns, knives, and plastic bombs. In September 1979, one such student riot was apparently sparked by a soccer match between rival schools at the national stadium. In what was reported by observers as an "orgy of violence," ninety-one students were arrested, several students were shot, and some policemen were injured.⁵³

The Reemergence of Student Activism

After the 1979 elections and a shift away from the conservative policies of Thanin to the more liberal regimes of Kriangsak Chamanand and Prem Tinsulamond, student leaders at some of the major universities began to resurface and promote political reforms. In the fall of 1979, a memorandum from student leaders at nineteen Thai universities was sent to Vietnamese Prime Minister Pham Van Dong protesting the exodus of refugees from Vietnam to Thailand.⁵⁴ This memorandum did not in any way oppose the Thai government and in fact supported the government's policy at the time. It was significant, however, in that student leaders were once again gaining visibility and beginning to articulate positions on political issues.

This strategy of using a mild form of political protest on a national policy issue had been used by NSCT leaders in November 1972, we recall, to mobilize students in a week-long Anti-Japanese Goods demonstration. That protest rally, which was also in keeping with the prevailing government sentiment, even gained praise from the Thanom government and the king. The major difference, of course, is that in 1972 the NSCT did much more than write a memorandum. The earlier student leaders of the NSCT seized the opportunity and gained national recognition by taking action through promotion of a boycott, protests, and demonstrations.

The new student leaders of the 1980s began their first demonstration in almost four years when two hundred university students protested a move by the military officers and politicians to extend the term of General Prem as army commander-in-chief. Normally in a civilian government this post is held not by the prime minister but rather by another person, usually a high-ranking military officer. The students protested that extending Prem's term as army commander-in-chief would lead to a revival of the "dictatorship" and martial law of previous Thai military governments. Major political parties, primarily the Democrat Party (Prachatipat), openly opposed Prem's extension, and the students became part of this traditional form of protest. After holding their protest rally, the students went to the Democrat Party headquarters to support parliamentary opposition to the extension.

About a month later, in December 1980, leaders of nineteen student unions joined representatives from the Labor Congress of Thailand (LCT) at the House of Representatives and formally recommended that the government reconsider the price of sugar, introduce clear and effective measures to stop hoarding, control the price of commodities, and announce a guaranteed just price for agricultural products.

Some weeks prior to the presentation of these recommendations to Parliament, students from Thammasat, Chulalongkorn, Mahidol, and Ramkamhaeng universities displayed placards at the Ministry of Commerce denouncing the "irresponsibility" of raising sugar prices. The students also planned an antigovernment campaign, but they called it off when Deputy Prime Minister Boonchu escalated his verbal offensive against them. Instead, Anuphap Choon-orn, president of the Thammasat University Student Union, decided that this student committee would "collect facts and data on the general economy and present them to the government's economic team for consideration."[55] When pressed by a reporter, Anuphap admitted that the strategy had been changed because "the students have no power to pressure the government."[56] The government responded to this more compromising approach in a positive way. The following month labor and student representatives were invited to the House Economic Commission meeting at the Parliament Building to discuss the LCT's recommendations to the government on economic issues.[57]

Hence the student leaders began to broaden their base for support among workers but kept within acceptable forms of opposition by bringing their grievances to Parliament. Throughout 1980 and 1981, student leaders continued to "use the system" by presenting their demands and grievances to the appropriate committees of Parliament.

The Revival of Direct Action

In April 1982, however, the students resorted again to direct action and began a protest demonstration at Government House on the issue of bus fares. The bus-fare issue had once before been a rallying point in 1969 when student leaders used it to mobilize students and workers against the government of Thanom. In fact, it was the bus-fare issue that helped give credibility and support to university students' political activities. Immediately after the student demonstrations succeeded in reducing bus fares to the original price in 1969, representatives of various universities met to establish the National Student Center of Thailand.

In keeping with the antimilitary tone of the new activism, student leaders from Thammasat and Chulalongkorn universities submitted a joint letter to Prime Minister Prem asking him not to choose his close associates and military officers to fill seventy-five newly vacated Senate seats. The letter warned that if General Prem continued to select senators from military circles and those close to him, "he would face more political upheavals."[58]

Just prior to that letter, students from four universities had gone to Government House with an open letter to Prime Minister Prem demanding a review of the bus fares, which had gone from one to two baht. By the end of the day, after vocational students chartered buses to join the gathering, the student protest group had grown to about three hundred. The activists threatened "strong action" by student leaders of all universities and labor unions to press the government for a reduction in the city bus fare.[59]

In the fall of 1982, student leaders began using new tactics such as prolonged sit-ins, hunger strikes, and other nonviolent means to get the government to negotiate with them on the bus-fare issue. In November a huge rally of three to four thousand people was organized by nineteen student unions and workers at Thammasat University to oppose the increase in bus fares.[60] At about the same time, however, another student group pledging opposition to the nineteen student unions emerged. The spokesman for this "loyalist student group," Samsak Kaewsakul, claimed that his group "represented the majority of the university students while the nineteen student unions represented the minority whose main purpose was to destroy the nation's economic system under the guidance of the country's enemy."[61]

At the end of November, the student activists began a hunger strike and sit-in at Government House. The students demanded to deal directly with Prime Minister Prem, rather than with his ministers, and set a deadline of 30 November at midnight. Pressure mounted as the hunger strike intensified and several labor unions joined in support of the students' demands. When Prem received reports that at least two of the hunger strikers were near death, he returned from the People's Republic of China where he was on an official mission.[62]

In a bizarre confrontation witnessed by the author, one of Prem's ministers maneuvered right up in front of the student leaders' podium at Government House in a small police car about one hour before the deadline. Never leaving the police car, he addressed the protesters through a microphone and student leaders responded in the same way—although the two parties were less than three feet apart. After several exchanges the minister apologized, explaining that Prem was still en route at Don Muang airport. More important, the minister explained that Prem had instructed him to inform the students and hunger strikers that the bus fare would be reduced and he would meet with the students and consider their demands regarding the removal of certain government transportation officials. Within the next two months Prem did follow through on most of these promises made to the students.

Some observers believed that the events in late 1982 were a genuine revival of the student movement and would eventually precipitate a coup. In an interview with the author in December 1982, however, Prime Minister Kukrit revealed that "those people who were threatening a coup were probably the same people who were behind the student activists in order to create the conditions for a coup." The following chapter places the 1975 and subsequent elections and the Thai Parliament in historical perspective while detailing the activities of the politicians associated with this important aspect of Thai politics as an oppositional force.

Notes

1. See Joseph Roueck, "The Political Role of Students in Underdeveloped Countries," *Comparative Education* 3 (March 1967):115–121.
2. This number does not include the police and military academies or NIDA, all of which represent institutions of higher learning that have as their specific purpose the training of prospective military and civilian government officials.
3. The present king resides in the New Palace about 3.5 kilometers from the Old Palace.
4. This territory is now part of Kampuchea and Laos.
5. *Bangkok Chronicle*, November 1940. The number of participants in one such demonstration was estimated at 400,000.
6. Pridi returned after having received a law degree from France and became the highest-ranking civilian in the 1932 bloodless revolution which usurped the power of the monarchy.
7. Prayat Sitiphan, *History of Thai Politics* (Dhonburi: Nakor Dhon, 1968), pp. 596–599.
8. Thereafter Pridi resided in the Peoples' Republic of China and was rumored to be the voice of the "Free Thai," a group of insurgents who proclaimed a government in exile and have vowed to return to liberate Thailand.
9. *Phimthai*, 12 October 1951, p. 1.
10. Most of this information was obtained through a personal interview with a former Thammasat student who participated in the entire affair.

11. In some provinces (Uttaradit, for example) the votes for the government exceeded the number of eligible voters.
12. Some Chulalongkorn students hung the flag on campus at half-mast designating the "death of democracy" in Thailand.
13. *Bangkok Post*, 22 June 1962, p. 1.
14. The announcement of the military government's decision to lift martial law in Bangkok was designed to reduce the pressure from opposition politicians who were testing the free-speech clause of the new constitution. For further details see Ross Prizzia, "Student Activism in a Comparative Perspective: The Political Participation of Thai University Students" (Ph.D. dissertation, University of Hawaii, 1971), chap. 3.
15. *Thai Rath*, 9 September 1973, p. 1.
16. *Bangkok Post*, 17 November 1972, p. 1.
17. *Bangkok Post*, 18 November 1972, p. 1.
18. *Bangkok Post*, 20 November 1972, p. 1.
19. Ibid., p. 1.
20. *Thai Rath*, 2 December 1972, p. 1.
21. *Bangkok Post*, 1 December 1972, p. 1.
22. *Bangkok Post*, 1 December 1972, p. 1.
23. Ibid., p. 1.
24. *Thai Rath*, 15 December 1973, p. 15.
25. *Bangkok Post*, 21 June 1973, p. 1.
26. Translated from a leaflet entitled "The Voice of the Students and the People," 21 June 1973.
27. *Bangkok Post*, 23 June 1973, p. 1.
28. Thirayuth Boonmee, "The Students Begin to Find Their Target," *Society of Students of Thailand*, July 1973, p. 3.
29. *Bangkok Post*, 23 June 1973, p. 2.
30. *Thai Rath*, 26 June 1973, p. 1.
31. *Bangkok Post*, 26 June 1973, p. 1.
32. Ibid., p. 1.
33. Thirayuth, "The Students Begin to Find Their Target"; translated from the Thai.
34. Ibid., p. 2.
35. Ibid., p. 3.
36. Although most political observers were caught unaware, all the ingredients for successful rebellion were there. In fact, all the data I collected in Bangkok during the summer of 1973—behavioral data on Thai students, a continuous file on student activism, and occasional rumors from university students in August—indicated the likelihood of a student uprising, a prediction I discussed at the time with disbelieving educators and colleagues.
37. Much of the information in this section was obtained from a special summary of "The Ten Days" compiled by the *Bangkok Post* and personal interviews with student leaders, members of the Crime Suppression Division, and various eyewitnesses and participants.
38. *Bangkok Post*, 10 October 1973, p. 2.
39. Seksan Prasertjul was at that time the public relations officer of the NSCT. In selecting the secretary-general of NSCT in July 1973, Seksan was also on the ballot, but he was narrowly defeated by Sombat Thamrongtanyawong of Kasetsart University. Seksan possessed great talent in public speaking and always

40. wore a hat like the one worn by Che Guevara, the Cuban revolutionary. Though many labeled him a radical, he was to emerge from this October uprising as a hero.
40. Later that day the king ordered the royal vehicles to take the students back to their homes safely.
41. The names of these three girls were never revealed, and some government officials claimed that no one was killed in this initial clash near the palace.
42. According to one report, tanks even pursued students in the presupposed safety of Thammasat University and fired into the campus grounds through the fences.
43. Government radio said that the rioters had plundered the gunshops. However, other sources said that the rioters had asked for only a few guns from each shop and the owners just gave the guns to them voluntarily. Some owners were said to have even demonstrated the proper loading techniques.
44. As reported by the *Bangkok Post*, 16 October 1973.
45. It was later revealed that Field Marshal Thanom flew to the United States, while Field Marshal Prapas and Colonel Narong went to Taipei.
46. According to the *Bangkok Post* summary the costs were great, as Bangkok hospitals were filled with the wounded. Public support was also great, however, as blood donations were so overwhelming that many hospitals ran out of containers.
47. The *Manhattan* was a United States warship of World War II stock which on 29 June 1951 was to be turned over to the Thai government. During the official ceremony aboard the ship, however, Prime Minister Phibun was kidnapped by navy officials who had long been disappointed with his policy of favoring the Thai army, police, and air force at the expense of the navy.
48. *Bangkok World*, 18 November 1973.
49. Ibid., 7 Jan 1974.
50. Ross Prizzia, "Thailand: Elections and Coalition Government (Part II)," *Asia Quarterly* 5(1976):281–285.
51. Ross Prizzia, "Thailand: New Social Forces and Re-emerging Socialist Principles," *Asia Quarterly* 4(1975):343–365.
52. Ross Prizzia, "Thailand: Elections 1979 and the 'New' Government," *Asia Quarterly* 2(1980):111–126.
53. *Bangkok Post*, 15 September 1979, p. 1.
54. *Bangkok Post*, 1 November 1979, p. 1.
55. *Bangkok Post*, 20 November 1980, p. 1.
56. *Bangkok Post*, 26 November 1980, p. 1.
57. Ibid., p. 1.
58. *Bangkok Post*, 13 December 1980, p. 1.
59. *Bangkok Post*, 22 April 1982, p. 1.
60. *Bangkok Post*, 3 March 1982, p. 1.
61. *Bangkok Post*, 30 November 1982, p. 1.
62. *Bangkok Post*, 30 November 1982, p. 2.

5
The Thai Parliament as an Oppositional Force

In our country the king is the one who takes the initiative, because he decides what should be done for the good of the country and the well-being of the people in general. This is contrary to the practice in any other country.... To conform with the way of the European kings in ruling over a country like Thailand is impractical. For example, if we establish a parliament, there will be few people who will be qualified as members; not all of them will understand governmental affairs, because they lack knowledge and obvious training. The people may be upset, because they do not understand; they think that this is unnecessary.

Thus spoke King Chulalongkorn, one of Thailand's greatest monarchs, and despite the passing of nearly a century, the king's comment would no doubt be held by many Thais to have the same validity today as it did in the nineteenth century. For amidst the swift current of events sweeping Southeast Asia, Thailand has attempted not only to cope with vastly changed external intricacies but simultaneously to continue its creation of a viable democracy.

This process of building a democracy, begun in earnest with the October 1973 overthrow of the Thanom Kittikachorn regime, has given rise to a situation in which the Thais may long for any sort of authority which takes the initiative and which can articulate and put into action a policy clearly for the well-being of the country and its people. Rather than a bright new world once the military retreated to the wings of the political process between 1973 and 1975, traditional values seem to have crumbled. And as King Chulalongkorn predicted, most of the populace were indeed upset, because they did not and for the most part could not understand the process of which they have become a part.

CONSTITUTIONALISM: POLITICAL PARTIES AND NATIONAL ELECTIONS

The periodic creation of political parties and national elections provides some basis for conventional types of political participation for the Thais. Participation in elections, however, except for a very small group of the voting Thai population, has been characteristically ceremonial in nature. This is especially true of the campaigning and elections which take place in the provinces.[1] Constitutionalism in Thailand, as elsewhere in transitional Southeast Asia, has served the country's political development by being a main element in the justification of political power.[2] It has also been a symbol of the process of admitting broader groups into the political process while allowing the ruling bureaucratic and royal elite to maintain their traditional status.

Constitutions, although manipulated and remade to serve the regime in power, have created several basic institutions that continue to have a certain vitality. With the nonpolitical king as a point of stability, the cabinet and national assembly are now, for the most part, established aspects of the Thai political system. National elections have been the most significant aspect of the development of constitutionalism and are usually carried out to meet specific constitutional provisions for the various national assemblies. The elections in April 1979 were the fifteenth in an irregular string of national elections together with various constitutions extending back to 1932.

The direct purpose of every election so far has been to return candidates to a national representative assembly. Legislative prerogatives are carefully limited, however, and political discussions have had little relationship to political decision-making. Participants in the House of Representatives have little realistic expectation of influencing events since elected representatives are balanced by appointed senators presumably loyal to the governing group.

This persistent presence of appointed members in every assembly since the first one in 1933 has characterized Thailand's political development as a "tutelary democracy."[3] The influence of an absolute, paternalistic government and autocratic bureaucracy cannot be underestimated; it has usually been reflected in the activities of the National Assembly, even though elected representatives did force three no-confidence votes upon the government between 1932 and 1939. This form of political action was successfully limited by the constitution of 1968, which prevented the House from calling a no-confidence vote at all. The 1974 constitution, however, reinstated this power to the House of Representatives. By 1970, Thai political parties were still in their beginning stages of development and were more like political clubs or parties of "individual representation."[4] Because of intervening periods of autocratic repression, political parties have not been active between elections, and only one, the Democrat Party, has maintained any continuity since its founding in 1946.

It should be noted that the Social Action Party established in 1974 and headed by Kukrit Pramoj and the Thai Citizens Party created in 1978 and headed by Samak Sundaravej have made significant gains at the expense of the Democrat Party. Both Kukrit and Samak were once leaders in the Democrat Party but broke away to form their own political parties.

Most parties are still the personal followings of individual leaders, or fronts for the autocratic cliques who control political power, and tend not to be ideologically oriented. Political interest and the political process are still a combination of many loosely related functions within Thai society. The representation of specific opinions and the aggregation of these opinions into sufficiently strong public demand for government action are concentrated within communal, personal, and social relationships.

Opposition groups face a pervasive belief by those in power that their independence will result in factionalism and separatism. In the past, opposition politicians' high-priced demands for cooperation with the government contributed to the charge of corruption and served to justify the coup d'etats between 1957 and 1971. The factionalism displayed during previous brief periods of political activity has continued to the present. The 1968 constitution provided less opportunity for democratic opposition to the government than previous versions, and the various restrictions became one of the centers of controversy between the ruling group and elected representatives that helped precipitate the coup of 1971.

The 1975 and 1976 elections, based on the relatively liberal constitution of 1974, provided the first coalition of opposition parties to take charge of the government. The civilian governments of both Seni Pramoj in 1975 and Kukrit Pramoj in 1976 were short-lived, however, and martial law replaced the fragile parliamentary governments after the October 1976 coup. The military has continued to resort to the coup when its interests are perceived to be threatened by any form of opposition, even in the absence of ideological contention in Parliament. The following analysis of the elections between 1969 and 1979, and the role of oppositional parties in the government formed after each election, must be placed within the perspective of Thai politics, which is dominated by military politics.

The 1969 Election

In 1969, as in 1975, there was a confusing array of candidates, including party members who attacked the other government candidates, independents who supported the government, and others who fit neither progovernment nor opposition groups. Although voters faced a difficult choice, it did heighten their interest in the elections.

The results of the 1969 elections established in the House of Representatives at least two opposition political groups: those who were elected as nongovernment candidates, about seventy-two in number, and the large group of seventy-two independent politicians who could be expected to support or oppose various government policies. The government party won about 35 percent of the seats: 75 out of 219. If the assembly was to function, the ruling group had to come to terms with one or both groups in order to gain support. The nongovernment political parties divided into two tentative positions: the Democrat Party and the Democratic Front Party.

The Democrat Party, with fifty-seven M.P.'s, had served as both government and opposition but campaigned in 1969 as a loyal opposition party. It had gained solid support in Bangkok, where the party won all twenty-one available seats, and it also won most of the seats in the northern provinces and a reasonable share in the northeast and south. The party members used good organization, campaigned on their policies rather than as individual candidates, and pledged to try to amend the constitution to make it more democratic. Thus they presented a conservative opposition, reasonably widely known and respected.

Close to the policy position of the Democrat Party was the Democratic Front Party, the third largest political party, which elected seven members. It claimed to possess a large party membership but nominated only fifty-four candidates. In parliamentary maneuvering after the election, the leader shifted his alignment away from the conservative Democrat Party toward more extreme splinter parties and interested independents. This group of non-aligned M.P.'s included about thirty members, approximately 50 percent from the smallest parties and the rest from the independent House members.

In 1969, opposition parties had criticized the constitution and during the campaign had promised to attempt its amendment. With this purpose in mind, the prime minister was questioned during the opening parliamentary debate on government policy. Visibly controlling his anger, Thanom stated that the constitution would not be amended since it was presented by King Bhumibhol to the people.[5] In later comments to the press, opposition politicians elaborated on their criticism that the government is not of the people until the elected representatives are allowed to decide on its legitimacy through a vote of confidence or no confidence.[6] Maneuvers among the extreme opposition aimed at unifying a position on a constitutional amendment proposal, along with other "unreasonable" demands by House members, eventually led to the 1971 coup which settled the constitutional issue by declaring martial law and dissolving Parliament.

THE 1975 ELECTION

The elections which took place in January 1975 were to be a significant departure from all previous attempts at parliamentary democracy in Thailand in that they were precipitated by a student-led civilian revolt. In the midst of the student and labor movements and increasing domestic trends toward socialism, however, it was the Phuu Ying Yai, "Old Important People," who resumed control of the government. There was, generally, a more liberal trend with a plurality victory for the old loyal opposition (Democrat Party) and a surprising number of seats (fifteen) for the new Socialist Party of Thailand. The military and industrialists reemerged with significant influence in the new government, however, as candidates associated with the old United Thai People's Party (UTPP), which had previously been led by the deposed Prime Minister Thanom, won more than a hundred seats under the banner of new party names. The four major parties backed by former UTPP members included the Social Justice Party which won forty-five seats, the Thai Nation Party with twenty-eight seats, and the Social Agrarian and Social Nationalist parties which won nineteen and sixteen seats respectively.

The problem of "independents" who had played a significant role in the 1969 and previous elections was solved by the 1974 constitution, which banned independent candidacies. This new constitutional provision—and the absence of a government party—encouraged the emergence of more than forty political parties, twenty-one of which won seats in the new Parliament. Moreover, the plethora of political parties produced Thailand's first coalition government—the viability of which became crucial to the success of the new Thai experiment with democracy.

In 1969, the third largest party had just seven members elected to Parliament; the 1975 elections resulted in nine parties with at least ten seats and seven parties with fifteen or more seats. Another significant difference was the trend toward socialism, as socialist parties won more than thirty seats in the new Parliament. Even the Democrat Party, which won a plurality of seventy-two seats, advocated "mild socialism" as the path out of Thailand's economic crisis.

The multitude of parties added confusion to the election process, even for the urban Thai in Bangkok. Although not all forty-two parties contested seats in all the provinces, the voter was confronted by more candidates and parties than ever before. In Ubon province, for example, ninety-five candidates representing more than twenty different parties ran for the nine available seats.

While there were many new candidates, familiar faces associated with the military and industry still appealed to voters in the provinces. Overall, about 50 percent of the candidates elected had been closely associated with the old military establishment; around 20 percent had won seats in previous elections under the former military party banner.

Seni Pramoj, leader of the Democrat Party and new prime minister, was burdened with the responsibility of forming a government. As Seni struggled over the terms of alliances with the leaders of loosely structured parties, the old UTPP groups began forming a cohesive voting bloc. Even though the Democrat Party won the most seats and had the apparent support of the liberal New Force Party and the leftist Socialist Party of Thailand and the United Socialist Front, it was the old UTPP M.P.s and their allies which emerged as the dominant force in the new Parliament under new Party banners.[7] After the new National Assembly convened for the first time to elect the speaker and deputy speaker, it became apparent that the "Allied Parties"—made up of several smaller parties and the Thai Nation, the Social Justice, the Social Agrarian, and the Social Nationalist Parties—significantly increased their influence in Parliament.

In attempting to seek a compromise within the House of Representatives, Seni was at first pressured by his leftist supporters to make a policy commitment of U.S. withdrawal from Thailand. The first policy statement to the public was that withdrawal would take place "as soon as possible." The next day, after much alarm expressed by supporters of the U.S. defense programs, this statement was changed to "withdrawal in eighteen months time." When reporters pressed Seni for an explanation of the sudden policy change, none was given. Thereafter, when Seni presented his government's policy package to Parliament, a no-confidence vote was requested by the opposition. The result was a 151 to 111 verdict which ended the brief tenure of the left-of-center coalition government. It is noteworthy that the heated debate which took place just before the crucial vote of no confidence centered on Seni's pledge in his policy manifesto that all foreign troops would be withdrawn in eighteen months.

There was considerable apprehension on the part of many Thais in Bangkok that the fall of the Seni government would provide an opportunity for the military to stage a coup. In an orderly manner, however, the members of the House of Representatives elected M.P. Kukrit Pramoj, leader of the Kit Sangkhom (Social Action Party), as prime minister to head the new government.

There was something characteristically Thai in making this selection. Kukrit, cousin of the king and Seni's younger brother, seemed to be a wise and safe choice. Though an outspoken critic of the military government for many years, Kukrit was also very critical of socialist-oriented policies. He had already served effectively as speaker of the House under Sanya's temporary government. As speaker he played a significant role in drafting the new constitution and the rules which guided the new Parliament. As leader of an aristocratic party supported primarily by bankers, Kukrit posed no serious threat to those of the upper and middle class who supported a capitalistic economy. As leader of the Social Action Party which secured only eighteen seats in the election, he posed no real threat to the military-backed parties. It was no surprise, then, when the military-backed parties joined in a coalition with the Social Action Party. Kukrit, unlike Seni, was not committed to a socialistic program of reforms; according to one report in a Thai newspaper, "even the CIA would not object to Kukrit as prime minister."[8] Although Kukrit's coalition government had to meet the challenge of new communist governments in Laos, Kampuchea, and Vietnam, as well as the internal problems of growing violence between new groups of militant rightists and leftists, he somehow managed to survive as prime minister until he was pressured to resign in early 1976. His departure prompted another election in April 1976.

THE 1976 ELECTION

Violence, which was primarily directed against socialist-oriented parties and candidates by various right-wing groups (NAVAPON, Red Gaurs, and others), did have an effect on the 1976 election results. Left-wing parties such as the Socialist Party of Thailand, the United Socialist Front, and the New Force, which together had captured thirty-seven seats in 1975, won only seven seats in 1976. Some parties on the right such as the Thai Nation doubled their 1975 seat total (from twenty-eight to fifty-six). This gain was mainly at the expense of their right-wing rivals, the Social Justice Party, whose seat total decreased from forty-five to twenty-eight, and the Social Nationalist Party which went from sixteen seats in 1975 to eight in 1976. Kukrit's own party increased its seat total from eighteen in 1975 to forty-five in 1976, but Kukrit lost his bid for a seat and any chance he may have had to lead the new coalition government. The biggest winner of 1976 was the Democrat Party, which captured a surprising 115 seats in the new Parliament—forty-three more than the seventy-two they had won in 1975. The Democrats' large plurality was the result of a sweep of the twenty-eight seats in Bangkok and strong support in the north, south, and northeast regions of the country. The Democrat Party captured seats in traditional socialist strongholds in the northeast as well as right-wing strongholds in the north and south.

The campaign violence perpetrated largely by the right, as well as the flood of Laotian, Kampuchean, and Vietnamese refugees who carried lurid stories of communist rule to the villages and towns of northeastern Thailand, were apparently important factors in the Democrats' victory. Voters seemed inclined to reject both extremes and opt for a return to the middle path.

Coalition Government Revisited

The overall election results meant that Thailand would have its second coalition government in scarcely more than a year. While the Democrat Party had won a convincing plurality of the vote, its 115-seat total was still twenty-five short of the majority needed to form a government. Thus the game of negotiations and compromise began once again, as various scenarios on possible groupings of parties were proposed.

The general feeling among most political observers was that the resulting coalition might be unstable, but it would be more stable than the preceding Kukrit coalition government if for no other reason than the fact that only four parties had any real bargaining power. It was generally surmised at the time that unless parties holding less than ten seats in the new Parliament formed an effective coalition, three of the four major parties (Democrat, Thai Nation, Social Justice, and Social Action) would most likely form a solid majority. The "Under Ten" coalition drive was a failure, however, and most of the candidates of these parties were forced to join in a loosely organized opposition with Kukrit's Social Action Party. After a week of negotiations, Seni Pramoj, leader of the Democrat Party, formed a coalition government with the Thai Nation Party (fifty-five seats), the Social Justice Party (twenty-eight seats), and the Social Nationalist Party (eight seats)—which represented a solid 206 of the 279 seats in Parliament.

The Issue of U.S. Troops

The status of U.S. troops, which was a factor in the demise of Seni's feeble coalition government in 1975, again became the major source of controversy surrounding Seni's 1976 coalition government. There was much speculation that Seni would reverse the order handed down by the previous government of Kukrit, which demanded that all American troops except 270 advisers leave Thailand by 20 July 1976. Prior to the 1976 elections, military leaders and various right-wing groups had demonstrated in support of a policy which kept at least four thousand U.S. troops in Thailand, while students and various left-wing groups held a series of anti-American protests to get all U.S. troops out of the country.

Some expected that Seni would at least modify the policy on U.S. troop withdrawals to approach a compromise between the forces on the right, some of which were part of his new coalition government, and those on the left. Instead, Seni held firm to the policy put forth by his younger brother Kukrit. Announcing his official decision in a formal address to the public, Seni emphasized that "the total withdrawal of American forces will be the right thing and a good thing in the furthering of peace in Southeast Asia." Moreover, Seni stated that removal of U.S. troops was in keeping "with the trend of the times" and this action did not necessarily mean that other powers would fill the vacuum created by the U.S. withdrawal. When Kukrit was asked to comment on Seni's surprising policy statement, as well as his own poor showing in the elections, the ever-witty former prime minister simply stated that he "wasn't surprised" by Seni's statement nor was he worried by his own election defeat because "after all, it's all in the family."

The Pramoj family arrangement notwithstanding, the Seni coalition government still faced critical social and economic problems which were left unresolved by the previous Kukrit government. Inevitably, in October 1976, the military again resorted to the coup and martial law and halted the demonstrations, riots, bombings, assassinations, and strikes which continued virtually unabated throughout Kukrit's tenure as prime minister and culminated in the bloody battle between government and students at Thammasat University.

THE 1979 ELECTION

After nearly three years of martial law, Thailand resumed its experiment with democracy and elected 301 candidates to the new Parliament in April 1979. As expected, Kriangsak Chamanand was retained as prime minister and head of the new Thai government. Kriangsak's success was the result of the solid support of the appointed senators comprising the upper house of the Thai Parliament. Although only 89 of the 301 popularly elected members of the House of Representatives supported Kriangsak, he was not required to share power in a coalition government as was the case in Thailand's two previous elections in 1975 and 1976. The difference was due largely to the special provisions of Thailand's tenth constitution, which was passed during martial law by the National Assembly and signed by the king in December 1978.

Many provisions of Thailand's tenth constitution were new only in the sense that they were absent from the relatively liberal constitution of 1974. Key provisions of the 1978 constitution were actually retrieved from the 1968 constitution drafted during the period of martial law under Thanom. While some Thai officials felt that the status-quo-oriented constitution was necessary to ensure a stable government, opposition political party leaders were particularly dismayed by the constitutional provision which gave the prime minister the power to appoint, with the king's approval, all 225 senators to the upper house of Parliament.

The 1979 election was characterized by low voter turnout due to the overall lack of enthusiasm generated by the campaign in general. Although the customary crowds would gather at the usual places to hear speakers from the various parties, there was a conspicuous absence of university students. In fact, students had assumed a low profile ever since October 1976, when the bloody battle with the police and right-wing groups at Thammasat University precipitated the military coup which eventually brought Kriangsak to power. The combination of the relatively noninvolved Thai middle class and apathetic students and intellectuals opened the door to the common poorer Thais (*phuu noi*) in Bangkok.

As election day approached, these *phuu noi* began attending rallies in greater numbers than ever. While election rallies of all parties had always been an inexpensive source of entertainment for many of the *phuu noi* of Bangkok, they were always followed by a particular pattern of voting that resulted in Thailand's oldest and most respected opposition political party, the Democrats, winning most or all of the seats in the capital. This had been the case in all three previous elections, and a similar pattern was being predicted by all the experts during the campaign.

They did not reckon on Samak, however, who broke away from the Democrat Party to start his own Thai Citizens Party and captured the imagination and votes of the *phuu noi*. Through astute oratory and techniques of mass appeal, he captivated the huge crowds at his rallies with a verbal barrage against Kriangsak, the Democrat Party, and the Social Action Party. The result was a surprising landslide victory for Samak and twenty-eight other Thai Citizens Party members in Bangkok. Thanat Khoman was the only member of the Democrat Party who managed to win a seat in Bangkok; the other two seats went to Kukrit and Dr.

Kasem, both leaders of the Social Action Party. Several virtual unknowns of the new Thai Citizens Party swept aside many prominent politicians and former government officials. The losers in Bangkok included Boonying, leader of the Freedom in Dharma Party (Seri Tham); Bhichai Rattakul, former foreign affairs minister; Damrong Lathapipat, former minister of commerce; and Chalermphan Srivikorn—all of the Democrat Party.

The defeat of the Democrat Party to the upstart Samak and his Thai Citizens Party in Bangkok was only the beginning of what was to become a complete collapse of the Democrats' strength throughout the country. As the results began to come in from the provinces, it soon became apparent that voters in the traditional Democrat Party strongholds had shifted to Kukrit's Social Action Party. The Social Action Party eventually won eighty-six seats in the provinces and eighty-eight seats overall.

Voter turnout in the provinces, at approximately 48 percent, was about the same as in previous elections and more than twice that of Bangkok. The low voter turnout was not a contributing factor in the demise of the Democrat Party, however. The Social Action Party's success in the provinces was due largely to the personal appeal of Kukrit, who gave numerous speeches in provincial towns in support of his party's candidates.

Kukrit's "Tamboon Fund," which began when he was prime minister in 1975, was a new plan for rural development that allowed farmers to borrow money from banks without collateral. This lending scheme enjoyed wide popularity among the farmers. Borrowing for agricultural pursuits required only a "character interview" and was designed to free farmers from loan sharks and high interest rates. Although the plan was not completely implemented and had only moderate success, Kukrit and his party's association with the fund became well known among farmers, who represent the majority of voters in the provinces. Moreover, Seni Pramoj's Democrat Party suffered from the usual complacency after the success of the 1976 election, as well as the misfortune of leading a seemingly powerless government when the military took over by a coup in October 1976.

The net result of the Democrat losses to the Thai Citizens Party in Bangkok and to the Social Action candidates in the provinces was a decrease in party strength in Parliament from 115 seats in 1976 to just 35 seats in 1979. Other new parties which benefited from the Democrats' collapse, as well as from their own organizational efforts in support of Kriangsak, were the Freedom in Dharma Party which gained twenty-six seats and the National Democrat Party which won ten seats. Several

Table 4
Comparison of Election Results: 1976 and 1979

Party	1976 B	1976 P	1976 T	1979 B	1979 P	1979 T
Isara (Independents)	—	—	—	—	41	41
Prachakonthai (Thai Citizens)	—	—	—	29	3	32
Seri Tham (Freedom in Dharma)	—	—	—	—	26	26
Prachatipat (Democrat)	28	87	115	1	34	35
Chart Thai (Thai Nation)	—	56	56	—	47	47
Kit Sangkhom (Social Action)	—	45	45	2	86	88
Dharma Sangkhom (Social Justice)	—	28	28	—	1	1
Sangkhom Chart Niyom (Social Nationalist)	—	8	8	—	—	—
Kaset Sangkhom (Social Agrarian)	—	8	8	—	8	8
Palang Mai (New Force)	—	3	3	—	8	8
Palang Prachachom (Populist)	—	3	3	—	—	—
Sangkhom Niyom (Socialist Party of Thailand)	—	2	2	—	—	—
Patthana Changwad (People Development)	—	2	2	—	—	—
Prachatippatai (Democracy)	—	1	1	—	—	—
Naewruam Sangkhom Niyom (United Socialist Front)	—	1	1	—	—	—
Pithakthai (Protect Thai)	—	1	1	—	—	—
Thai Sangkhom (Thai Social)	—	1	1	—	—	—
Dharmathippatai (Merit Is Right)	—	1	1	—	—	—
Sangkhom Kaona (Progressive Social)	—	1	1	—	—	—
Siam Mai (New Siam)	—	1	1	—	—	—
Naewruam Prachathippatai (United Democracy Front)	—	1	1	—	—	—
Rang-ngarn (Labor Party)	—	1	1	—	—	—
Chart Prachachon (National Peoples)	—	—	—	—	10	10
Ruan Thai (Thai Unification)	—	—	—	—	2	2
Kit Prachatipathai (Democrat Action Group)	—	—	—	—	2	2
	28	251	279	32	269	301

B: Bangkok; P: provinces; T: total.

"old" parties also gained in strength even though some of their leading members lost in their bid for reelection. Such was the case with Dr. Krasae, leader of the New Force Party, who lost in his bid for a seat in Khon Kaen even though his party increased its strength to eight seats. The Thai Nation Party decreased its seat total only slightly from fifty-six in 1976 to forty-seven in 1979. Other smaller parties such as the Social Agrarian Party (Kaset Sangkhom) remained the same as in the last election with eight seats.

Complete results of the 1979 elections in Bangkok and the provinces as well as a comparison with results of the 1976 elections are shown in Table 4. In all, forty-one independents won seats, many of whom eventually formed the basis for a Kriangsak-supported coalition with the Freedom in Dharma Party and other smaller parties in the House of Representatives. As expected, Kriangsak became head of the new government after he was nominated to that post in a special session of Parliament. Kriangsak received only 89 of a possible 301 votes from the elected members of the House of Representatives. The bulk of his votes came from members of the Senate (222 out of 225), all of whom he had appointed only months before.

The call for a special session by Kriangsak resulted in a boycott by the four major parties in the House: the Social Action Party, the Thai Nation Party, the Democrats, and the Thai Citizens Party. Therefore Kriangsak's successful nomination was marred by the absence of nearly 200 of the 301 elected M.P.'s.

The timing of the special session remained a much debated issue among the opposition parties and was even referred to as "a plot to create enemies and topple the government itself" by Social Action leader Kukrit Pramoj.[9] In a much calmer atmosphere, Social Action's deputy leader, Boonthing Thongswat, was unanimously elected speaker of the House. With Kukrit's deputy in control of the House and the Social Action Party forming the basis for opposition to Kriangsak and his hand-picked Senate, the lines for future conflict in the new government were already drawn.

THE "NEW" GOVERNMENT

While the SAP-led opposition was able to exercise some leverage regarding future policy matters, its influence in the formation of a new government was almost nil. Its weakness was due largely to the limitations placed on the elected M.P.'s by the 1978 constitution. In the 1975 and 1976 elections, a coalition of various members in the House comprised a majority and therefore had the right to form a new government. The 1978 constitution prevented a majority of the elected M.P.'s in the House from forming the government, however, and instead required a majority of the entire Parliament including the appointed Senate. The new constitution also allowed the prime minister to select members to the cabinet with only the approval of the president of Parliament, who was also the speaker of the Senate. According to the new constitution, cabinet members did not have to be selected from elected M.P.'s as was required in all previous constitutions. Thus the new constitution's emphasis on the appointed Senate and the speaker of the Senate in the formation of the new government not only paved the way for Kriangsak as prime minister but also provided him with a rubber-stamp approval process in the selection of his cabinet.

While there still existed hard bargaining for cabinet seats among Kriangsak's supporters (such as the Freedom in Dharma Party), the disruption which characterized the haggling for positions in the three previous coalition governments was greatly reduced. This change was due not only to the absence of a coalition government but also to the fact that the constitution enlarged the cabinet to forty-four posts and therefore provided Kriangsak with more seats with which to reward his supporters.

In the months immediately following the 1979 elections and the formation of the new government, a more liberal trend evolved as labor and other groups began pressuring Kriangsak for reforms. In the meantime Kukrit, relying on his widespread popularity and wit, undermined Kriangsak's efforts to increase support for his military-dominated government among the elected M.P.'s. In July, only three months after the election, Kukrit managed to rally the House unanimously to censor Kriangsak for not replying to Parliament's proposal for reforms. Kriangsak, conscious of his dwindling popularity, made a series of concessions to government and private labor organizations on wage adjustments and bonuses and changed several aspects of the Labor Law. He also signed into law several of Parliament's proposals which deleted the discriminatory "alien father" clauses of the Election Bill and repealed the infamous "danger to society" bill which had allowed the arrest and indefinite detention of anyone regarded as "dangerous" without due process.

The delicate balance of the Kriangsak government shifted dramatically only ten months later when, in February 1980, a series of controversial oil price policies resulted in a near no-confidence vote in the House and Kriangsak's resignation. General Prem Tinsulamond, a friend and advocate of the royal family, agreed to form a new government. Prem replaced the military-dominated cabinet, including the position of deputy premier, with respected civilians such as Boonchu Rojanasathien and Thanat Khoman. By choosing talented civilians and familiar military leaders, Prem hoped to increase the likelihood of solving Thailand's crucial economic problems and to win a broader base of support in the House of Representatives.

But Prem, the honest and capable military leader, was unable to transfer his skills of leadership to the position of prime minister. Expected to solve problems of inflation, corruption, rural underdevelopment, and the like, he instead displayed an ineptness for making decisions on any of these critical issues. His attempt at "consensus" by distributing cabinet posts among the major coalition parties—Social Action, Thai Nation, and the Democrats—created bitter party rivalry. In March the Social Action Party quit the coalition after sharp disagreement with the secretary-general of Thai Nation, who was the agricultural minister. Prem's hesitance on critically needed social and economic programs and his aloofness with regard to the open rivalry among his cabinet members prompted impatience and finally a coup in April 1981 by the Young Turks of the Thai military.

The coup of April 1981, which was led by Gen. Sant Chitapatuma and masterminded by Col. Manoon Rupekachorn, both of the prestigious First Army in Bangkok, lasted less than three days. The traditional takeover by the First Army in Bangkok, which was usually followed by the commanders of the Second and Third Armies in the provinces, did not occur. Instead King Bhumibhol, in an unusual move, gave support to his friend Prem by flying to Korat where the Second Army was based. This move prompted most of the military forces to remain loyal to the Prem government. The Young Turk faction, not wanting to engage in an actual battle in opposition to the king's apparent choice, disbanded in favor of Prem's countercoup after several tense hours of a standoff between the two military factions.

Prem returned as prime minister in the midst of mixed loyalties among many military officers. He offered amnesty to the coup leaders but stripped them of their military status, replacing them with officers who had remained loyal during the coup. Prem also reshuffled his cabinet to reward loyal factions of the military, including the right-wing extremist Maj. Gen. Sudsai Hasdin. The aftermath of the abortive coup gave rise to a staunchly military-dominated government with a volatile but powerless parliamentary opposition led primarily by Samak and his Thai Citizens Party.

The 1983 Election and Coalition Government

Throughout 1982 the military continued to maneuver in order to consolidate its position in the Prem government, while the diverse political parties campaigned in preparation for elections scheduled for spring 1983. As was the case prior to the 1979 elections, there was again widespread speculation that the military would stage a coup to stall or even prevent the elections.

Instead, the military-backed politicians made several vain attempts to change various election rules which threatened to reduce the role of the armed forces in future Thai governments. Moreover, Army Commander-in-Chief Arthit and several other officers among the military elite attempted unsuccessfully to pressure Parliament to repeal several democratic reforms in the new constitution that were scheduled to take place after the 1983 elections. These reforms were part of a

"Twelve-Year Plan for Democracy" that was to begin with the 1979 elections and culminate with the 1987 elections when all democratic reforms (such as an elected Senate) were to be in place.

From its inception few political observers believed that the plan for increased democratic reforms and successive orderly elections every four years would succeed without being interrupted by a military coup. Prior to the 1983 election, however, the reform-oriented politicians and parties prevailed and prevented the various maneuvers on the constitution attempted by Arthit and his followers and at least stalled what some Thai politicians referred to as the military's attempt at a silent coup.

The 1983 elections were held as scheduled in April with more than 53 percent of the eligible voters going to the polls.[10] The voter turnout was the second largest in Thai history and was to some extent due to the widespread publicity of the military's various attempts to alter the election rules and repeal the democratic reforms of the new constitution. The overall effect of these political maneuvers apparently assisted many of the reform-oriented politicians and parties in the election.

The Social Action Party under Kukrit's leadership increased its strength in Parliament by five seats and led all other parties with ninety-three seats, while the Democrat Party led by Bhichai increased its elected M.P.'s from thirty-five in the 1979 election to fifty-six M.P.'s in 1983. The Thai Nation Party led by General Pramarn won seventy-three seats in the new Parliament, an increase of twenty-six from the 1979 election. Opposition leader Samak also increased the Thai Citizens Party's strength from thirty-two seats to thirty-six.

Because none of these parties enjoyed an absolute majority among the 324 seats in the lower house, a coalition government of two or more of these major parties seemed inevitable. At first it seemed that the Democrat, Social Action, and Thai Nation parties would form the new coalition. After several weeks of negotiation and speculation, however, the Social Action, Democrat, and Thai Citizens parties joined with the newly formed National Democracy Party, which had won fifteen seats, to form a coalition government with a solid majority of 261 seats. To the surprise of most Thai political observers this left the military-backed Thai Nation Party in the role of the opposition. It also resulted in a 44-member cabinet dominated by elected civilian representatives and led by Prem, who was invited to continue as prime minister as well as defense minister.

The election results and the formation of the civilian-dominated cabinet were seen by many Thais as a major step toward the development of democracy in Thailand. The military leaders, Arthit in particular, did not abandon their attempts to repeal various constitutional reforms in order to safeguard the role of the military in future Thai governments, however, and it seems likely that if the military is not accommodated Arthit may resort to a coup or some other means to gain greater control for the military in the new government.

NOTES

1. See Herbert P. Phillips, "The Election Ritual in a Thai Village," *Journal of Social Issues* 14 (4) (1958): 37.
2. See Seymour Martin Lipset, "Party Systems and the Representation of Social Groups," in Avery Leiserson (ed.) *Political Parties and the Study of Politics* (New York: Knopf, 1958), p. 44.
3. For discussion of the potential impact of legislatures on democratic development see Robert B. Stauffer, "A Legislative Model of Political Development," *Philippine Journal of Public Administration* 11 (January 1967): 3–12.
4. See Sigmund Neumann (ed.), *Modern Political Parties: Approaches to Comparative Politics* (Chicago: University of Chicago Press, 1956), p. 404.
5. *Bangkok Post*, 25 March 1969.
6. *Bangkok Post*, 28 March 1969.
7. See *Bangkok Post*, 28 January 1975, p. 1.
8. *Ban Muang*, 21 May 1974; editorial about Kukrit when he first formed the Kit Sangkhom Party.
9. *Asia Week*, 25 May 1982, p. 16.
10. On 20 March, in a move which surprised many of the party leaders, the king in conjunction with Prime Minister Prem signed a royal decree dissolving Parliament and calling for an election on 18 April—about two months earlier than the originally scheduled date of 12 June. In effect this meant that the elections would be held under the existing traditional electoral system with voters picking individuals in multiple constituencies instead of single constituency party slates in the winner-take-all system that was to take effect on 21 April 1983. Hence the transitory clause of the new constitution creating a single constituency for each province, which was designed to increase the strength and influence of the established political parties, was postponed until the next election.

   Another important transitory clause designed to further democratic reform of the military-dominated Senate did take effect on 21 April 1983, however. The constitutional change meant that the 225 appointed senators who had traditionally sat in joint sessions with the lower house and often determined the outcome on critical legislative issues (for example, no-confidence matters) were prohibited from such joint sessions after 21 April 1983.

6
The Meaning of Thailand's Transition

Theoretically the shift in Thailand's foreign and domestic policy might best be represented in terms of its economic and political system. There is little doubt that the predominant economic system, adopted primarily from the United States, was based on a scheme of monopoly capitalism. This infusion of Western capital—either directly from a foreign government to the Thai government or indirectly through multinational corporations, which in some cases maintained 100 percent ownership (Firestone, Toyota, and others)—was readily accepted by many of the Thai government's leaders (Sarit, Phibun, Thanom) to be the proper path to economic development. Moreover, achievement of economic development along these lines presupposed an advance in political development as well. It was generally believed that the necessary ingredients of political development (national integration, national consciousness, democratic institutions, political participation, and so forth) would somehow evolve as a result of economic development.

While Thailand's economy was in fact developing by commonly accepted criteria (such as GNP), particularly under the authoritarian regime of Field Marshal Sarit Thanarat, political development lagged far behind and, some scholars maintain, even declined.[1] There is also some question as to whether the overall goals of economic development were achieved. Along these lines the overall efficacy of the so-called dependency model of development—which assumes that priming the needy pumps of developing nations such as Thailand with various and continued external resources will eventually create self-sufficiency—needs to be reevaluated.

Typical of the incongruities created by external assistance to overall national development is the case of the Bhumibhol Dam in Tak province. This project is located in a remote area of rural Thailand and began with elaborate designs that would provide not only irrigation for agricultural purposes but also electricity for rural households in the area. The irrigation aspect of the plan was never fully implemented, however, and huge cables carried the dam's energy output to provincial capitals and Bangkok while most of the villagers in the immediate vicinity of the dam remained without electricity or easy access to water. Such examples of the inequitable distribution of national resources are characteristic of the consequences of the dependency model of development as it was applied to the authoritarian regimes in Thailand and other countries in Southeast Asia.

The student revolution of 1973 which overthrew the Thanom military regime forced open the Thai political system and allowed—if not by design then at least by consequence—the participation of previously locked-out groups representing various sectors of Thai society. By the spring of 1975, in fact, protests by various groups of students, workers, and farmers had become a common, if not legitimate, form of political participation. The predominantly socialistic orientation of the leaders of many of the protest groups gave rise to speculation that these movements were being infiltrated by "foreign communist elements."

My purpose here is neither to support military speculation of communist infiltration in the social movements in Thailand nor to lend credence to the socialist cause. Rather I wish to present an overview, through historical analysis, of the transition in the context of the unprecedented events reflected in the student, worker, and communist movements and the reemergence of the Thai Parliament. It is from this perspective that I want to clarify the implications of Thailand's transition.

The articulation of demands by these new interest groups revolved around a variety of basic structural changes in the Thai political arena. During this period (1973–1976), most of their demands were at least temporarily met by the Thai government. In meeting many of these demands (for wages, land, and political enfranchisement, for example) the government's transactions frequently represented only the allocation of certain resources to groups who were previously denied access to them. In other cases, however, the transactions represented a significant transfer of power—the power to review, investigate, and initiate policy—to groups (students, workers, farmers, and others) who were rarely, if ever, involved in the policymaking process. The overall impact of the politics of confrontation on the Thai political economy had only begun to be felt by the Thai elite during this transitional period.

The drama, tension, and subsequent negotiated settlement that characterized each direct confrontation with the Thai government elite were fast becoming the *modus operandi* for all groups seeking remedial action for their grievances. Although a parliamentary process had miraculously evolved from the chaos of this transitional phase of Thai politics, the spokesmen for the new interest groups rarely worked through their representatives and usually bypassed Parliament entirely in achieving concessions directly from the Thai government. Moreover, as soon as one group was accommodated by the government, another group, as if by chain reaction, would initiate the customary phase of mobilization, articulation of demands, and confrontation.

The Essence of the Transition

At the height of the drama surrounding a series of demonstrations involving workers, farmers, teachers, students, and even some radical right-wing organizations, one Thai offical remarked, "It's as if the ground has begun to swell up around us." That remark, though made lightheartedly at the time, may very well epitomize the essence of Thailand's transition during this period.

This historically significant time in Thai history was characterized by unprecedented movements generated from below—that is, at the very foundation of the Thai political system. It was not in any sense a full-blown *batiwat chownaa* (peasant revolution), but it was characteristically different from all previous shifts in the Thai political system, such as Chulalongkorn's "adjustment" to the colonial appetites of the British and French from 1890 to 1910, the so-called 1932 revolution involving the overthrow of the monarchy, and the events of 1940–1946, involving the much publicized "shifty Thai politics" during and after the Japanese occupation of Thailand. These illustrations are typical of the classic style of political change in Thailand, which had always taken place from above.

The grass-roots movements in Bangkok and the provinces involving the *phuu noi* (common people) provided some evidence to those who proposed that Thailand had, in the aftermath of the student revolution of 1973, given rise to a "new democracy." Moreover, the socialist orientation assumed by many of the leaders of these movements further supported this notion. This ideological orientation toward socialism, while not new to Thai politics, underlies another basic distinction between this transition and all previous periods of political change in Thailand.

Pridi Panomyong adhered to socialist principles and actually attempted to institute several socialist-oriented policies during his brief tenure as prime minister in 1946. His ill-fated plan for political change was activated in characteristic fashion from above, however, and was neither well received nor even understood by those who were supposed to be its main benefactors. Moreover, Pridi's socialistic plans for political change were characteristic of "bourgeoisie socialism" involving a shift of power from the military to the educated civilian elite in implementing change for the masses. His plans while prime minister did not call for grassroots movements initiated and carried forward by the *phuu noi* themselves.

The Role of the Military

The role of the Thai military during this transitional period was one of "watchful waiting" while indulging in behind the scenes political maneuvers affecting the new Parliament and coalition governments. Although various military cliques did create political parties and field candidates which they lavishly supported in political campaigns, this transitional period was marked by an unusual degree of fragmentation in the ranks of all three branches of the armed services and among the various levels of Thai police.

There had always been tension between the various branches of the Thai armed services and the police, but tension within each branch of the armed services was a new phenomenon. Cleavages were particularly evident in the Royal Thai Army and the Thai police—between the old entrenched officers, on the one hand, and the younger officers (Young Turks) and new cadets on the other. There was an increase in tension and, in some cases, a complete breakdown of lines of authority between ranking officers from comfortable elite backgrounds and new officers from modest origins.

One important factor which led to vertical cleavages was the growing communist threat in the provinces during this period, a threat which necessitated the relocation of many ranking officers from their customary comfort in Bangkok to remote areas. Customarily the new recruits and young officers from nonelite backgrounds were sent to these areas to engage the communists in battle while the so-called crack army divisions led by officers of elite backgrounds remained in Bangkok. The Thai military elite's preference for Bangkok was based on more than a liking for safety and comfort; it was also the most effective path to upward mobility within the military system. A Thai army officer achieved promotion by finding and serving a high-ranking patron—and by being in Bangkok when the next military coup took place—and not through heroic efforts in battles against the communists. There is a well-known saying about the Thai military's pattern of succession since Field Marshal Phibun became prime minister after a successful coup: "*Sarit maa jaak Phibun, Thanom maa jaak Sarit, le Kris maa jaak Thanom.*" That is, Prime Minister Sarit came from his patron Phibun, Prime Minister Thanom from his patron Sarit, and so on down to present Prime Minister Prem and his commander-in-chief of the Thai army, Arthit Kamlang-ek.

THE LIKELIHOOD OF ANOTHER COUP

Although the preceding chapters have focused on Thailand's "new left" perhaps at the expense of more conventional aspects of Thai politics, it should be noted that a persistent fear of a military coup was evident throughout the initial transition period (1973–1976). Constant rumors about the military's plans to return to power circulated throughout Thailand during this period and were particularly pervasive in the months of June and November 1974. A brief military alert after the resignation of Prime Minister Sanya Thammasakdi in June 1974 gave rise to speculation of a return to military rule, but Sanya was persuaded to resume office and, in doing so, rid the cabinet of most of the military officers left over from the Thanom regime. A three-day battle with the police in Bangkok's Chinatown in November precipitated another general military alert, but Field Marshal Kris vowed that he "would not be the one to perform a coup," even though he admitted that some officers wanted to make the move to "preserve order." There was a rumor of a coup following the collapse of Seni Pramoj's coalition government in February 1975, but this event did not even precipitate a military alert.

The power vacuum left by the military in the wake of the student revolt of 1973 was filled only briefly by the students, and the military remained a powerful influence in Thai politics during this period of transition. Communist offensives in the spring of 1975, which led to communist governments in neighboring Kampuchea, Vietnam, and Laos, caused considerable apprehension among many military leaders. This series of events—combined with the growing domestic upheaval among Thai workers, farmers, and students and increasing demands by members of the new Socialist Party of Thailand—seemingly provided a deterrent to any plans for a military coup.

Why was there no coup after October 1973? The reasons are not entirely clear. Several members of the Socialist Party maintained that it was primarily factionalism within the military ranks that had stalled a coup; it would come, they said, as soon as the military leaders became properly unified. On the surface the military seemed content to work through the Kukrit coalition government in accommodating the domestic social forces and in pursuing a policy of rapproachement with the

People's Republic of China and the new communist governments of Vietnam, Kampuchea, and Laos.

During this period Kukrit played an active role in establishing Thailand's international priorities in accordance with the realities of the politics of détente in Southeast Asia. Thailand's new priorities included an exchange of ambassadors with the People's Republic of China and diplomatic initiatives to the newly formed communist governments of Laos, Kampuchea, and Vietnam as well as a shift away from what many Thais considered to be a neocolonial relationship with the United States.

Events after the successful student uprising of October 1973 did stimulate the growth of several right-wing organizations. These groups were, and still are, led primarily by the traditional Thai elite. The most notable among these groups which openly opposed the leaders of students and workers was the Right-Wing Protest Group (Phitak Chart Thai). The Phitak Chart Thai held several rallies in May and June 1975 in Bangkok to warn the Thai people about the left-wing groups who were "ruining the country." Therdphun Chaidee, leader of the hotel workers union, and student leaders Seksan Prasertjul and Thirayuth Boonmee were the prime targets of the angry speakers, who referred to them as "communists" and "Reds." One speaker for the Phitak Chart Thai, Phan Visut, blamed Therdphun, Seksan, and Thirayuth for the unrest in the country—and urged his audience "to get rid of them." Phan said in one of his speeches that he was particularly upset with the un-Thai-like behavior of these "barbarians" in a protest at the U.S. embassy, who had torn the eagle out of the embassy's plaque and replaced it with a drawing of a vulture.

The Phitak Chart Thai rallies were poorly attended. The first rally at the Sanam Luang grounds was greeted with catcalls and even stones, forcing the speakers to flee from the speaking platform (which happened to be the roof of a truck). Other rallies were without incident as they were afforded the protection of the Kitin Daeng (Red Gaurs or Red Bulls), a militant right-wing youth group which became a prominent factor in subsequent elections and the 1976 coup.

Other less militant right-wing organizations such as the NAVAPON were somewhat more successful in obtaining public support, particularly among the Thai upper class. This organization, named in honor of the Nine Chakri Kings, was established to preserve and promote the institution of the monarchy and maintain traditional patterns of respect for all Thai institutions. The spokesmen for these right-wing groups were basically pro-American and anticommunist—and were well funded by wealthy Thai businessmen. These groups were rather ineffective in their purpose of swaying the workers, farmers, and intellectuals away from the growing socialist trends, however. The Kukrit government and the Thai bureaucracy continued to avoid confrontation by appeasing the new forces on the left. After October 1973, most of the demands of all major protest movements by students, workers, and farmers were eventually met by the government. In short, this period represented an unprecedented proliferation of interest groups in Thai politics. The prospects of some of the new groups improved at the expense of old established groups. While violent confrontation between these old and new forces was for the most part avoided, the prospects for a stable government and a lasting parliamentary democracy remained doubtful.

As expected, the coup did come. In October 1976, after a series of violent clashes between militant forces of the right-wing Red Gaurs and leftist students and workers that finally culminated in a two-day battle involving police and special military commando units on the grounds of Thammasat University, the military took over the reins of government. On the surface, the threat from the leftist-oriented social forces seemed at least temporarily eliminated.

There was a certain irony about the coup which finally took place on 6 October 1976: Both the military establishment and the extreme left (the Thai Communist Party) seemed to have achieved their ultimate goals. On the side of the military, many of the younger cadets and the middle-level officers (Young Turks) under the domination of the Thanom–Prapas clique had often voiced their distress that former Prime Minister Thanom and his deputy Prapas were exceptionally corrupt during their period of tenure and had remained too long. What these military officials were suggesting in a sense was that the military establishment needed an overhaul. There needed to be new blood, new life, and a new source of energy to run the country via a military government. On the other hand, certain Marxist-oriented groups wished to divide the country along rightist and leftist ideologies.

In 1972, except for members of the National Student Center of Thailand, very few Thai students possessed what one might call a political consciousness at all. Certainly no potential seemed to exist for an extreme Marxist perspective. But the events of 1973 and the transition period that followed, 1973 to 1976, allowed several socialist-oriented groups, even extreme Maoist factions, to enjoy considerable success among students, workers, and farmers and also among intellectuals at the major universities in Bangkok, particularly at Thammasat and Chulalongkorn. The promotion of Marxist economics became quite commonplace from 1974 to 1976 on these campuses. Even some traditionally conservative parties in the elections of 1975 and 1976 expressed a desire to include a mild socialist platform among their other promises.

The events leading up to the takeover by Defense Minister Sangna showed how successfully the leftist tactics and polarization really worked when former Deputy Prime Minister Prapas attempted to return home from exile in Taiwan. The most visceral of the left and right factions battled openly in the streets with guns, grenades, and other weapons. The return of Thanom from exile in Singapore saw these events not only repeated but reaching more violent heights which eventually precipitated the coup in October 1976. The leftists who had continually raised the specter of oppression and militarism were in a sense proved correct, as civilians witnessed the bloody battles of Thammasat University and swift repression by the new military government which included the arrest of thousands of students, hundreds of intellectuals, and even the prime minister himself. In the meantime the Thai Communist Party, aware of the Thai government's vulnerability owing to the political upheavals in Bangkok and new demands by Laotian-speaking northeastern Thais and various other politically isolated groups (Meos and others), increased supplies of arms, weapons, and ideology to these groups. The new communist regimes in Laos, Vietnam, and Kampuchea also began to step up their support for guerrilla movements in the north and northeastern regions of Thailand.

The suppression of all forms of opposition by the Thanin government from 1976 to 1979 merely increased the growth of the communist movement. The proliferation of CPT front organizations included hundreds of former members of the student, worker, and farmer movements and even several former members of the disbanded Socialist Party of Thailand. The invasion of Vietnam by China and the subsequent split between Chinese and Vietnamese factions of the CPT caused a serious dilemma for CPT leadership, however, resulting in a dramatic loss of membership and effectiveness in 1980.

The military politics of the abortive coup of April 1981 resulted in the weakening of several key military commands in rural Thailand through the removal of capable Young Turk officers on the list of General Sant's supporters and their replacement by Prem loyalists. Moreover, some of Prem's most capable officers (such as General Pichit) were shifted from the battle front to the First Army in Bangkok. This temporary disorganization in the Thai military ranks may give the CPT strategists the reprieve they need in view of the dramatic losses they have suffered on both the political and military fronts since 1980.

Ironically, the viability of the Thai Parliament may well depend upon the continued success of military-backed parties such as the Thai Nation in the House to protect the military budget and other interests. The Thai labor movement as well as the entire economy are affected by military politics, which protects its corporate interests through membership on various boards of directors and constrains labor disputes through control of key positions in the cabinet (the Ministry of Interior, for example). As long as Thai politics remains military politics, legitimate oppositional forces such as the Parliament and labor union movements will only be as influential as the prevailing military leadership will tolerate.

If significant splits in the military such as the Young Turk upheaval continue to occur, various oppositional forces may temporarily benefit from the rivalry among the military leaders. Yet none of these oppositional forces except Kukrit's Social Action Party, or to a lesser degree the Thai Nation or Democrat parties, could possibly fill the vacuum through democratic processes while only the CPT, with possible Vietnamese backing, stands ready to fill the vacuum through force. The latter scenario seems unlikely so long as the CPT Central Committee remains dominated by Chinese-trained leaders and the dispute between China and Vietnam continues.

THE 1983 ELECTION AND BEYOND

The various political party leaders readied themselves for the April 1983 elections amid rumors that a coup by General Arthit was inevitable. One concern was the new election laws that provided for winner-take-all in each district by the political party whose candidate received the most votes. It was widely believed, as the political campaigns began to unfold in 1982, that Kukrit's Social Action Party would be the main benefactor of the law.

Another concern of the military-backed government was the growing support for an elected rather than an appointed upper house in Parliament, which was in accordance with the "Twelve-Year Plan for Democracy" that was officially enunciated during Thanin's regime in 1976. Any move to limit this means for direct military involvement in the Senate was seen as a threat to the military itself.

A third concern was the reemergence of student activism in the fall of 1982 as student activists from Thammasat and Ramkamhaeng universities began to mobilize, protest, and demonstrate in a manner reminiscent of the early 1970s. In the fall of 1982, a student protest and hunger strike at Government House eventually led to various concessions by the Prem government which included the reduction of the bus fare in Bangkok.

Some observers believed that the events in late 1982 were a genuine revival of the student movement and would eventually precipitate a coup. In an interview with the author in December 1982, however, Kukrit revealed that the student movement seemed to be more contrived than real; he suggested that certain military leaders (such as Arthit) were the primary benefactors.

The results of the 1983 elections seemed to provide Kukrit and his Social Action Party the opportunity to play a central role in the civilian-dominated cabinet of the new coalition government. While Kukrit and other politicians maintain that the Thai parliamentary process is genuinely evolving to the point of becoming an integral and permanent institution in Thai politics, there always remains the possibility that the military may again opt for a coup or some other tactic to safeguard its role in the Thai political process.

International events in Southeast Asia as well as domestic political developments in Thailand in spring 1984 seemed to lend credibility to Thai fears regarding the threat of Vietnamese forces along the Thai borders and the growing influence of the Thai military in Parliament.

On the international front, Vietnamese forces took the offensive against the various factions of the anti-Vietnamese coalition operating in Kampuchea and along the borders of Thailand and The People's Republic of China. The Vietnamese offensive included an assault against the Chinese-backed communist forces of the Khmer Rouge near Thailand's Sisaket Province in the northeast as well as attacks on the Thai backed non-communist forces of the Khmer People's National Liberation Front (KPNLF) and the Armée Nationale Sihanoukiste (ANS) of Prince Norodom Sihanouk.

The Vietnamese offensive spilled over into Thailand and Yunnan and Guangxi provinces in southern China. Inevitably, Thai and Chinese military units became involved in a number of battles with the Vietnamese forces in March and April of 1984. The Thai military amassed over 10,000 of its best troops to stop the Vietnamese incursions and claimed a major victory at Phra Palai Pass where, according to Thai sources, over two hundred Vietnamese troops were killed as opposed to only ten Thai troops. Meanwhile, after a week of intense shelling of each other's positions along the Chinese-Vietnamese border, a Chinese regiment reportedly crossed the border, overran and briefly held several strategic hilltops in Vietnam's Long Son Province.

On the domestic political scene in Thailand, Arthit and his followers continued their attempts to increase military influence in the Parliament and undermine opposition to military-backed proposals. Newspapers in March 1984 carried full coverage of criticisms of members of Parliament by Arthit who maintained that most M.P.'s are elected by a populace that does not have a full understanding of democracy. In apparent agreement with Kukrit on the subject, Arthit argued that an understanding of democracy is a key to national security. Arthit followed his verbal attacks on various M.P.'s with another concerted effort to change the 1983 transitory clauses of the constitution which had reduced the power of the appointed senate in the Thai Parliament.

The necessity for civilian-dominated governments to accommodate the military in order to assure stability and longevity was poignantly recognized by Kukrit himself in an interview in which he sarcastically argued that the military was "unfortunately misunderstood" and there was "no danger" from them. "When I was prime minister," he said, "I stood to attention every time a general came in to see me and that worked very well...."

NOTES

1. See, for example, Frank C. Darling, *Thailand and the United States* (Washington, D.C.: Public Affairs Press, 1965).

Index

Absolute monarchy, 38
Anti-American activities, 73–75, 91–94, 108
Anti-Communist Laws: Law of 1933, 9–11; effect on labor, 26
Anti-French demonstration of 1940, 41
Anti-Japanese Goods Week, 50–52
Anti-military student activities, 42–43. *See also* Student activism, Student Revolt of October 1973
Arbitration and Thai legislature, 32
Army, Thai: and occupation of Thammasat University, 42–43; and Pridi's coup in 1949, 42; and "Ten Days," 69, 70, 71. *See also* Military role in government; Young Turks
Arthit Kamlang-ek, Commander-in-Chief, 100, 101, 107
Article 17, 62
Article 21, 33, 36n.8
Association of Communist Youth of Siam, 7
Association of Tramway Workers, 26

BATU. *See* Brotherhood of Asian Trade Unions
BMTA (Bangkok Mass Transit Authority), 34–35
Bang Khen, Metropolitan Police Training School and Detention Center at, 61, 63, 65
Bangkok: anti-Phibun demonstrators, 44; BMTA strike, 34–35; closing of universities, 63; location of universities, 40–41
Bangkok Federation of Trade Unions, 26
Bangkok Mass Transit Authority. *See* BMTA
Bhichai Rattakul, 96, 101
Bhumibhol, King of Thailand: and Student Revolt of October 1973, 68, 70; support for Anti-Japanese Goods Week, 51–52; support for Prem, 100; and Thanom's resignation, 70. *See also* Monarchy as National Institution
Blacklists by students, 72
Boonchu Rojanasathien, 99
Boonsong Chalethorn, 60
Boonthing Thongswat, 98
Boonying (leader of Seri Tham Party), 96
Brotherhood of Asian Trade Unions (BATU), 29
Bunpod Bintason, 54
Bureaucracy, Thai: autocratic, 87–88; reforms in, 2–3, 72. *See also* Democratic elective process
Bus fares, 45–46, 83; and student activism, 81–82
Business, Thai and government, 33

CCPDF (Committee for Coordinating Patriotic and Democratic Forces), 20–21
CCPT (Chinese Communist Party of Thailand), 10
CIA (Central Intelligence Agency), 74–75; anti-Kinter protests, 73–75; phony letter to Prime Minister Sanya, 74–75; rela-

tions with Thailand (before 1975), 75
CPM (Civil-Police-Military), 22
CPT (Communist Party of Thailand) 7–24; cadres, recruitment and training, 13–15, 24–25; China's role, 13–15; Chinese-Vietnamese factions, 21–22; elimination of class distinction, 16–18; establishment, 7, 10–11; future of, 110–111; influence of Ho Chi Minh, 7–8; North Vietnam's role, 15–20; after Coup of 1976, 33, 79; Thai Liberation Organization and "Peace Revolt," 10–11. *See also* Anti-Communist laws, Farmers' Liberation Organization
CSOC (Communist Suppression Operations Command), 11, 62, 64, 65
Cabinet, Thai: and labor disputes, 32; and 1983 election, 101; and political system, 87
Central Intelligence Agency. *See* CIA
Central Labor Union, 26–27
Chai Suwansnasorn, Maj. Gen., 65
Chaiwat Suravichai, arrest of, 60, 64
Chalermphan Srivikorn, 96
Chiang Mai University, 12, 39, 53, 55
Chief Justice of the Supreme Court, 52–53
Chinese Communist Party of Thailand. *See* CCPT
Chulalongkorn, the Great King. *See* Monarchy as National Institution
Chulalongkorn University: administrators accused of corruption, 46–47; anti-Phibun demonstration, 43–44; history, 38–40; interuniversity member, 48; Marxist economics, 109; 1959 coup, 42. *See also* Student Revolt of October 1973
Civil service employees, 31–32. *See also* Bureaucracy, Thai
Civilian governments, 72, 79, 86, 101
Civilian workers strikes and NSCT, 71
Coalition governments, 86, 90, 93; in 1975, 90–91; in 1976, 93; in 1983, 101. *See also* Kukrit Pramoj; Seni Pramoj
Collective bargaining: reasons for failure, 32; success, 35–36
College of Education, 38, 40
Committee for Coordinating Patriotic and Democratic Forces. *See* CCPDF
Commodity prices, 81
Communism: Chinese, 7; Vietnamese, 7–9

Communist insurgents in Sakhon Nakhon. *See* CIA: phony letter to Prime Minster Sanya
Communist Operations Suppression Command. *See* CSOC
Communist Party of Thailand. *See* CPT
Constitution: and constitutional activists, 63, 65, 67; of 1968, 55, 87–88, 89–90; and Coup of 1971, 50, 88; of 1974, 88, 90; Tenth Constitution (1968), 33, 94–95, 95, 98–99. *See also* Freedom of assembly
Constitution of the National Student Center of Thailand. *See* NSCT: constitution of
Constitutionalism, 87
Coup d'etats: between 1957–1971, 88; lack of, between 1973–1976, 112–113; speculation of, in 1982, 83
Coups: of 1932, 2; of 1947, 42; attempted in 1949, 42; of 1959, 42; of 1971, 50, 90; of 1974, 77; of 1976, 12, 94, 109–110; of 1981, 100
Courts, labor. *See* Labor courts
Courts, Thai: and Decree 299, 52–53; and labor disputes, 32

Damrong Lathapipat, 96
Damrong, Prince, 2
"Danger to Society" bill, repeal of, 99
Deaths during demonstrations. *See* Police brutality
Decree 299, 52–53
Democracy Development Program, 77
"Democracy," definition of transitional, 5
Democracy Monument: building of, 40; site of student demonstrations, 54, 55–56, 65, 67, 70
Democrat Party: establishment, 88; in 1969 election, 89; in 1975 election, 90–91; in 1976 election, 92–93, 96; in 1979 election, 95–96, 98; in 1983 election, 101
Democratic elective process, 72–73
Democratic Front Party, 89
Democratic Patriotic Front, 12
Demonstrations. *See* Protest marches and demonstrations
Dependency model of development, 103–104
Direct action, revival of, 81

"Dirty Election." *See* Elections, of 1957
Domestic policy reforms, 1–2, 3

Elections, 87, 97; "Alien Father" repeal, 99; of 1957, 43; of 1969, 89–90; of 1975, 31, 90–92; of 1976, 31, 92–94; of 1979, 34, 94–98; of 1983, 100–102, 102n.10, 111
"Executive Decree," 33

FIST (Federation of Independent Students of Thailand), 3, 30, 76. *See also* Free Thammasat Movement
FWAT (Free Workmen's Association of Thailand), 27
Farmers' Liberation Organization, 11, 18; as CPT front organization, 19
Farmers and "Tamboon Fund," 96
Farmers Party, 79
Federation of Independent Students of Thailand. *See* FIST
Foreign policy reforms, 3–4
France, cession of eastern territory by, 41
Free Thai Movement, 9, 42. *See* Pridi Panomyong
Free Thammasat Movement, 73. *See also* Seksan Prasertjul
Freedom of assembly, 60; Article 17, 62; Article 21, 33, 36n.8

General Labor Union, 26
Government, paternalistic, 87
Government House, 82, 111
Grass roots movements, 105
Gray Organization, 11
Gun battles between students and police. *See* Police brutality

Ho Chi Minh, 7–8
Hoarding, measures against, 81
Hotel Labor Federation of Thailand, 34
Hotel Workers' Union, 31. *See also* Chaidee Therdphun
House Economic Commission, 81
House of Representatives, 87, 89
Hunger strikes by students: over bus fares, 82; and constitutional activists, 63

Import quotas and student demands, 75
Independent candidates, role of, 89, 90, 97, 98
Independent Chulalongkorn Student Group, 73

Japan: occupation during World War II, 42; student demands of Tanaka, 75; trade with Thailand, 50–51. *See also* Anti-Japanese Goods Week; Free Thai Movement
Jen-Min-Jih-Pao (newspaper), 14
"Jit" (Thai revolutionist), 68
Judges of Labor Court, selection of, 33
Justice Act of 1952, 52, 53
Kampansan district (Nakonpathom), interuniversity meeting, 48
Kampuchea and World Court decision, 44–45
Kasem, Dr., 95–96
Kasetsart University: establishment, 38; location, 40; interuniversity meeting, 48; new system, 72
Khaisaeng Suksai, arrest of, 62
Khananum Thai (Thai Youth Group), 9
Khao Praviharn (temple), 44
Khonkaen University, 39
Kings of Thailand. *See* Bhumibhol, King of Thailand; Monarchy as national institution
Kinter, William R., 73–75
Krasae, Dr., 97
Kriangsak Chamanand: comparison with Thanin regime, 21, 80; election, 94, 96–98; and labor strikes, 34–35; laws and bills passed, 99; resignation, 99
Kris Sivara, 62
Kukrit Pramoj: anti-American proposal, 3; coalition government (1973), 3–4; coalition government (1975), 78–79, 91–92; home looted, 32; interview with Prizzia, 83, 112; resignation and 1976 election, 92, 93, 94; and Social Action Party, 88; "Thamboon Fund," 96; wins seat (1979), 96, 99
Kularb Saipradit: arrest of, 11; exile, 14; political asylum, 12; writings, 14
Kuomintang. *See* Nationalist Chinese Party

Labor and Kriangsak, 99
Labor Congress of Thailand (LCT), 33, 34, 81

Labor Court, 33, 34–35
Labor Department and BMTA strike, 34
Labor disputes and legislation, 31–36
Labor Law of 1956, 27–28
Labor Law of 1971 and Thanom, 28
Labor leaders, arrests of, 33–34
Labor Reform Bill of 1978, 33–34, 36
Labor Relations Committee, 34–35
Labor unions, 26–36; history of labor movement, 26–27; influence of military government, 110, 111; minimum wage law, 28, 30–31, 32; 1976 coup, 33; no enforcement of labor laws, 32; Textile Workers' Strike, 31, 32. *See also* Strikes
Laborer, Thai. *See phuu noi*
lang kru, 73
Leaflets: seizure of Constitutional leaflets, 60; support for Ramkamhaeng Nine, 54; support for students by civilians, 55; use by labor unions, 32
Left, The New, 4
Legislative Council and Decree 299, 53
Legislature and arbitration, 32
Letter from CIA agent. *See* CIA: phony letter to Prime Minister Sanya
Loans from Japan and student demands, 75
"Loyalist Student Group," 82

MIT. *See* Movement of the Independence of Thailand
MWWA (Metropolitan Water Works Authority), 34, 35
Mahachon (The Great Mass) (newspaper), 10
Mahidol University, 38, 39, 40
Manhattan (ship) affair, 85n.47
Manoon Rupekachorn, Col., 100
Maoist Movement, 4, 11
Martial law: from 1958 to 1969, 45; after 1976 coup, 94; proclaimed by Sarit, 44; proclaimed by Thanom, 50
Metropolitan Police Headquarters, burning of, 70–71
Metropolitan Police Training School, 63
Metropolitan Water Works Authority. *See* MWWA
Military role in government, 71, 77; future role, 100, 111. *See also* Young Turks
Military and police, 106–107
Minimum wage law, 28, 30–31, 32

Minister of Justice and Decree 299, 52–53
Ministries of Labor and Industry, 32
Ministry of Agriculture, 38
Ministry of Education, 38
Ministry of Public Health, 38
Monarchy as national insitution, 66, 76, 87; absolute monarchy, 38; King Chulalongkorn on monarchy, 86; protesters' loyalty, 58, 66, 76. *See also* Bhumibhol, King of Thailand
Monchai Phankongchuen, 68
Monkon Nonakon, 14
Montri Juengsirinarak, 60
Movement for the Independence of Thailand (MIT), 13, 14
Muanchom Risapda (Masses Weekly) (newspaper), 9

NA. *See* Nonaligned unions
NAVAPON, 92, 108
NCTL (National Council of Thai Labor), 33–34
NFWC (National Federation of Workers Congress), 33, 34
NLDAC (National Labor Development Advisory Committee), 33
NSCT (National Student Center of Thailand), 37, 47–50; Anti-Japanese Goods Week, 50, 58; bus fares, 81–82; constitution of, 48; organization, 48–49; splinter groups, 76; and student activism, 37, 47, 57–58; Student Revolt of October 1973, 60, 61, 65–67; Teaching Democracy Program, 4, 76–77; Textile Strike, 30
naa tii (duty), 31
Nakornsawan, 43
Narong, 85n.45
National Assembly, 87, 91; House of Representatives and Senate in, 87
National Council of Education, 38–39
National Council of Thai Labor. *See* NCTL
National Democrat Party, 96
"National Emergency," 43, 44
National Executive Council: and Anti-Japanese Goods Week, 52; and freedom of assembly, 52, 60; and Thanom, 50
National Federation of Worker Congress. *See* NFWC
National Institute of Development Administration, student organization and

"Ten Days," 61
National Labor Development Advisory Committee. *See* NLDAC
National labor federations, 33
National Student Center of Thailand. *See* NSCT
National Thai radio station, 42, 53
Nationalist Chinese Party, 7
Navy: and 1959 coup, 42; and "Ten Days," 71
New Force Party, 79, 92, 97
Newspapers, 74; *Bangkok Post* and "Ten Days," 84n.37; Communist, 8, 9, 10, 14; *Siam Rath*, 24n.4, 75–76
Nine Ramkamhaeng University Students. *See* Ramkamhaeng Nine
No-confidence vote, 87–88, 91
Nonaligned unions (NA), 33, 34
Nopporn Suwanpanich, 60
Northeastern province, 74
"Old Important People" (*phuu ying yai*), 90
Old Palace, 40, 42
"Open arms" program and CPT defections, 22

PDG. *See* People for Democracy Groups
PLAT. *See* People's Liberation Army of Thailand
Paisarn Tawatchainand, 34
Parliament: and military, 77, 110; after 1971 coup, 50; after 1979 election, 96–98; and Thammasat University, 42–43
Parliament Building and student protests, 40
"Peace Revolt" and Thai Liberation Organization, 11
People for Democracy Group (PDG), and textile strikes, 30
People's Liberation Army of Thailand (PLAT), 19
People's Republic of China, 3, 82
Pham van Dong, 80
Phayom Chulanond, 14–15
Phibun Songkram: anti-American Prime Minister, 9; Coup of 1947, 10; and students, 43, 44; and trade unions, 27–28
phuu noi (common laborers), 4, 31, 95, 105–106
phuu yai (superiors), 31

phuu ying yai (old important people), 90
Police and "Ten Days": Crime Suppression Division, 55; halted buses, 52, 54; and demonstrations, 65, 68–71
Police brutality, 68–71
Political parties: characteristics, 88, 97. *See also* Democrat Party; Election; Social Action Party
Prachuab Suntharangkoon, Lt. Gen., 60
Prakob Charumanee, Maj. Gen., 64
Pramain Ground: location, 40, 41; site of demonstrations, 31, 43, 45, 52, 53, 54
Pramarn, Gen., 101
Prapansak Komolpetch, 60
Prapas Charusathien, Gen.: and "Ten Days," 51, 60, 62, 63; as director general, 70; flees to Taipei, 85n.45
Prasammitra Teachers College, 48, 62
Preedi Boonsue, arrest of, 60
Prem Tinsulamond, Gen.: and bus fares, 82, 83; Coup of 1981, 100; government, 80, 99; "open arms" program, 22; retained after 1983 election, 101; student protests against, 80–81, 82, 83
Pridi Panomyong: flees to China, 83n.8; and Free Thai Movement, 9, 14, 42–43; overthrow of monarchy, 8–9, 42, 83n.6; Prime Minister, 105–106; writings, 14
Prime Minister, Office of: and student marches, 44, 46–47, 52, 53; and universities, 38
Prime Minister's Office Organization Act of 1963, 38, 39
Protest marches and demonstrations 31, 63; Bangkok routes, 40–41. *See also* CIA; Ramkamhaeng Nine; Student Revolt of October 1973
Puay Ungphakorn, Dr., 9

Rachan Wiraphan, 65
Rajdamnern Avenue: buildings set afire, 69–70; location, 40, 41; and "Ten Days," 65, 68–70
Ramkamhaeng Nine, 54–55; university expulsion, 56–57; sentence changed to suspension, 57
Ramkamhaeng University: establishment and location, 40; policies, 53–54
Red Guars (Kitin Daeng), 92, 108–109
Red Organization, 11

Reforms, transitional, 2
Right-wing organizations, 79, 108–109
Rond Thasanachalee, resignation of, 72

SAP. *See* Social Action Party
Sakdi Phasooknirand, Dr., 54, 57, 58
Samsak Kaewsakul, 82
Sant Chitapatuma, Gen., 100, 110
Sanya Thammasakdi, 70, 72, 74, 79
Samak Sunderavej, 95, 100
Sarit Thanarat: abolished Labor Law of 1956, 28; and coups, 12, 44
Satjang (Truth) (newspaper), 9
Secondary schools and protests, 63
Seksan Prasertjul, 20, 25n.22, 76–77, 84n.39, 108; leader of FIST, 73, 76; and Student Revolt of October 1973, 67, 69
Senate, 87
Seni Pramoj: coalition government, 79; leader of Democratic Party, 91, 96; proposes withdrawal of U.S. troops, 91–92, 93–94
Seri Tham Party, 96, 97, 98
Serm, Gen., and BMTA strike, 34
Siam Communist Committee, 9
Siam Rath (newspaper), 75, 76
Silapakorn University, 38, 39, 40
Snan: labor leader of BATU, 29; secretary-general of NCTL, 34
Social Action Party (SAP): establishment, 92, 93; 1979 election, 95–96, 97, 98; government (1980), 99–100; 1983 election, 101
Social Agrarian Party, 90, 91, 97
Social forces, emergence of, 2–3
Social Justice Party, 90, 91, 92
Social Nationalist Party, 90, 91
Socialism, 91, 105–106
Socialist Party of Thailand, 79, 90, 92
Songkla Nakarin, University of, 39
State Railway of Thailand (SRT), 35
Strikes: BMTA and other government workers, 34–35; and National Labor Development Advisory Committee, 33; outlawed, 33; student absences in strikes, 35; teachers, 29; textile workers' strike, 30–32; wildcat strikes and "Ten Days," 71
Student activism: and absolute monarchy, 38; in 1969 election, 48; occupation of Thammasat campus, 42–43; reemergence (after 1979), 80, 82–83, 111, 112; "Ten Days" and effects, 3, 9, 109, 110. *See also* Student demonstrations
Student demonstrations: anti-French demonstration of 1940, 41; anti-Japanese demonstration, 50–52; Chulalongkorn administration, 46–47; Decree 299, 52–53; "Dirty Election" of 1957, 43–44; martial law and bus fare increase, 45–46, 82; occupation of Thammasat campus, 42–43; World Court, 44–45. *See also* CIA; NSCT; Ramkamhaeng Nine; Student Revolt of October 1973
Student Front, 55
Student Revolt of October 1973, 1, 2–3, 59–72; and CPT, 20; arrests and imprisonment of constitutional activists, 61–65; led to 1975 coup, 90; military and police violence, 65–71; resignation of Thanom announced by King, 70; summary, 71–72, 104. *See also* NSCT; Seksan Prasertjul; Thanom Kittakachorn; Thirayuth Boonmee
Sudsai Hasdin, Maj. Gen., 100
Sukdi Pasuknirunt, 36n.1
Summit Oil workers and strike, 35
Sunam Luang, 35

TCP (Thai Communist Party), 9, 10
TLO (Thai Liberation Organization), 11
TNTUC (Thai National Trade Union Congress), 27
"Tamboon Fund," 96
Tanaka, Prime Minister, 75
Teachers Training College, and protest, 63
Teaching Democracy Program, 4, 76–77
Telephone Organization of Thailand (TOT), 35
"Ten Days." *See* Student Revolt of October 1973
Textile Workers' Strike, 30–32
Thai Afro-Asian Solidarity Committee, 15
Thai Citizens Party, 88; in 1979 election, 95–96; in 1981 election, 98, 100; in 1983 election, 101
Thai Communist Party. *See* TCP
Thai Liberation Organization. *See* TLO
Thai Nation Party: in 1975 elecltion, 90,

INDEX

91; in 1979 election, 97, 98; in 1983 election, 101
Thai National Legislative Assembly (NLA), 33
Thai National Trade Union Congress. *See* TNTUC
Thai Patriotic Front (TPF), 13, 19; "Six-Point" program, 18
Thai Youth Organization, 11
Thai People's Liberation Army, 22
Thailand Federation of Patriotic Workers, 15
Thailand Federation of Trade Unions, 15
Thammasat University, 39, 40, 65; anti-French demonstration, 41; closed after military occupation, 42–43; defiance of martial law, 45; Marxist economics, 109; "Ten Days," 61, 63; 1976 coup, 20, 33, 94. *See also* Therdphun Chaidee; Pridi Panomyong
Thanat Khoman, 95, 99
Thanh-Ai (Friendship) (newspaper), 8
Thanin: and CPT, 21; shift from conservatism, 80; strikes outlawed, 33–4; and students, 79
Thanom Kittikachorn: Anti-Japanese Goods Week, 51; constitution and "Ten Days," 46–47, 50, 61; downfall of government, 59, 70, 71; Labor Law of 1971, 28; leaves country, 71, 85n.45. *See also* Student Revolt of October 1973
Thanya Chunkathatharn, arrest of, 60
Thawee Muenthikorn, arrest of, 60
Therdphun Chaidee, 108; and CPT, 20, 22; and Hotel Workers' Union, 31
Thirayuth Boonmee: and CPT, 20, 22, 25n.22; and NSCT, 49–50, 58, 59, 60, 61
Thongpak Priangvat, 21
"Tutelary Democracy," 87
"Twelve-Year Plan for Democracy," 101, 111

24 Mithuna (newspaper), 9

UTPP. *See* United Thai People's Party
Union of Motor Tricycle Drivers, 27
United Nations, 10
United Professional Workers' Union, 11
United Socialist Front, 92
United States of America, 9, 10, 12, 74. *See also* CIA; Seni Pramoj
United States National Labor Relations Board, 33
United Thai People's Party, 90
University Council, 47

VLO (Volunteer Liberation Organization), 12
Vasit Dejkunchorn, 68
Vietnam and refugees, 80
Vietnamese Communist Party, 7–8
Violence in demonstrations: Anti-Japanese Goods Week, 50; avoidance (1957), 44; 1976 election, 92; Ramkamhaeng Nine, 54; "Ten Days," 68–69, 70–71
Volunteer Liberation Organization. *See* VLO
Voters, 87, 96, 101

World Court, 44–45
Worker movement, 26–36; Labor Reform Bill of 1978, 33–36; student role, 29–31; support for students, 44, 66–67, 71; Textile Workers' Strike, 30–32
World University Service, 48

Yellow Organization, 11
"Yellow Tigers," 70
Young Turks: faculty members, 55; military dissidents, 100, 109, 110

Index preparation by Susan Elliott Miller, Diane Sakai, Hewitt Reynolds, and Arlene Seto Ching, with special thanks to Professor Sarah K. Vann, University of Hawaii Graduate School of Library Studies.

About the Author

Ross Prizzia is associate professor of political science and public administration at the University of Hawaii at West Oahu College. He was the primary author of *Thailand: Student Activism and Political Change* (1974) and coauthored in Thai *The Prospects for Democracy in Thailand* (1975). He was also author of the Thai edition of *Mobilization of the "Phuu Noi" and the Future of Thailand* (1975) as well as numerous journal articles on oppositional forces in Thailand. His research, which was supported by the East-West Center, the University of Hawaii Research Council, and other institutions, has focused on the Communist Party of Thailand, students, farmers, workers, and other political movements in Thailand. Results of his research have been presented through guest lectures at the National Institute of Development Administration's Graduate School of Public Administration, at Thammasat University in Thailand, and at various state, national, and international conferences.

Asian Studies at Hawaii

No. 1   *Bibliography of English Language Sources on Human Ecology, Eastern Malaysia and Brunei.* Compiled by Conrad P. Cotter with the assistance of Shiro Saito. September 1965. Two parts. (Available only from Paragon Book Gallery, New York.)

No. 2   *Economic Factors in Southeast Asian Social Change.* Edited by Robert Van Niel. May 1968. Out of print.

No. 3   *East Asian Occasional Papers (1).* Edited by Harry J. Lamley. May 1969.

No. 4   *East Asian Occasional Papers (2).* Edited by Harry J. Lamley. July 1970.

No. 5   *A Survey of Historical Source Materials in Java and Manila.* Robert Van Niel. February 1971.

No. 6   *Educational Theory in the People's Republic of China: The Report of Ch'ien Chung-Jui.* Translated by John N. Hawkins. May 1971. Out of print.

No. 7   *Hai Jui Dismissed from Office.* Wu Han. Translated by C. C. Huang. June 1972.

No. 8   *Aspects of Vietnamese History.* Edited by Walter F. Vella. March 1973.

No. 9   *Southeast Asian Literatures in Translation: A Preliminary Bibliography.* Philip N. Jenner. March 1973.

No. 10 *Textiles of the Indonesian Archipelago.* Garrett and Bronwen Solyom. October 1973. Out of print.

No. 11 *British Policy and the Nationalist Movement in Burma, 1917–1937.* Albert D. Moscotti. February 1974.

No. 12 *Aspects of Bengali History and Society.* Edited by Rachel Van M. Baumer. December 1975.

No. 13 *Nanyang Perspective: Chinese Students in Multiracial Singapore.* Andrew W. Lind. June 1974.

No. 14 *Political Change in the Philippines: Studies of Local Politics preceding Martial Law.* Edited by Benedict J. Kerkvliet. November 1974.

No. 15 *Essays on South India.* Edited by Burton Stein. February 1976.

No. 16 *The* Caurāsī Pad *of Śrī Hit Harivaṁś*. Charles S. J. White. 1977.
No. 17 *An American Teacher in Early Meiji Japan*. Edward R. Beauchamp. June 1976.
No. 18 *Buddhist and Taoist Studies I*. Edited by Michael Saso and David W. Chappell. 1977.
No. 19 *Sumatran Contributions to the Development of Indonesian Literature, 1920–1942*. Alberta Joy Freidus. 1977.
No. 20 *Insulinde: Selected Translations from Dutch Writers of Three Centuries on the Indonesian Archipelago*. Edited by Cornelia N. Moore. 1978.
No. 21 *Regents, Reformers, and Revolutionaries: Indonesian Voices of Colonial Days, Selected Historical Readings, 1899–1949*. Translated, edited, and annotated by Greta O. Wilson. 1978.
No. 22 *The Politics of Inequality: Competition and Control in an Indian Village*. Miriam Sharma. October 1978.
No. 23 *Brokers of Morality: Thai Ethnic Adaptation in a Rural Malaysian Setting*. Louis Golomb. February 1979.
No. 24 *Tales of Japanese Justice*. Ihara Saikaku. Translated by Thomas M. Kondo and Alfred H. Marks. January 1980.
No. 25 *Mandarins, Gunboats, and Power Politics: Owen Nickerson Denny and the International Rivalries in Korea*. Robert R. Swartout, Jr. March 1980.
No. 26 *Nichiren: Selected Writings*. Laurel Rasplica Rodd. 1980.
No. 27 *Ethnic Groups and Social Change in a Chinese Market Town*. C. Fred Blake. 1980.
No. 28 *The Evolution of Hindu Ethical Ideals*. S. Cromwell Crawford. 1982.
No. 29 *Experimental Essays on Chuang-tzu*. Edited by Victor H. Mair. 1983.
No. 30 *Songs of Nepal*. Siegfried Lienhard. 1984.
No. 31 *The Origins of Japan's Modern Forests: The Case of Akita*. Conrad Totman. 1985.

Orders for Asian Studies at Hawaii publications should be directed to the University of Hawaii Press, 2840 Kolowalu Street, Honolulu, Hawaii 96822. Present standing orders will continue to be filled without special notification.